T0293893

FICTIONAL LONDON

FICTIONAL LONDON

A GUIDE TO THE CAPITAL'S LITERARY LANDMARKS

STEPHEN HALLIDAY

First published 2013 as *From 221B Baker Street to the Old Curiosity Shop*
This edition published 2020

The History Press
97 St George's Place, Cheltenham,
Gloucestershire, GL50 3QB
www.thehistorypress.co.uk

British Library Cataloguing in Publication Data.
A catalogue record for this book is available from the British Library.

ISBN 978 0 7509 9405 7

Typesetting and origination by The History Press
Printed and bound in Great Britain by TJ International Ltd.

CONTENTS

Introduction

London's place in literature is unrivalled. From Chaucer's pilgrims gathering at the Tabard Inn, Southwark to the Hogwarts Express departing from Platform 9¾ at King's Cross, it has proved endlessly tempting to novelists, poets and others whose imaginations have woven the great city into their stories; its streets, parks, squares, buildings and, of course, its river have featured in more works than it is possible to mention. Even its weather has appeared in some works where London's sinister 'smog' (dense fog impregnated with smoke) has appeared not just as an element of the tale, but almost as a character in its own right. It would be possible to devote a whole volume to London's place in the books of a number of individual writers who have used London as a backdrop to many of their works. Charles Dickens and Arthur Conan Doyle come into this category and their characters are to be found in many different parts of London, not least because they often make quite long journeys; Sherlock Homes and Dr Watson travelling by carriage while Dickens's characters are often obliged to make the journey on foot. According to his friend and first biographer, John Forster, Dickens loved walking around London and became a familiar figure to passers-by. In Forster's words:

> To be taken out for a walk in the real town, especially if it were anywhere about Covent Garden or the Strand,

> perfectly entranced him with pleasure. But most of all he had a profound attraction of repulsion to St Giles's. If he could only induce whomsoever took him out to take him through Seven Dials he was supremely happy.

Seven Dials, the seven-way junction at the top of St Martin's Lane, was once in the centre of London's most infamous slum tenements. It can still be visited and is now in the heart of London's entertainment district where visitors and theatregoers walk without anxiety, unaware of its fearful history.

Dickens walked almost every day, sometimes as much as 20 miles at a time. This habit, and his consequent familiarity with London's streets, no doubt accounts for the detail with which Dickens describes the journeys of characters like Oliver, as he is led to Fagin by the Artful Dodger, and Bill Sikes as he flees to Hampstead after killing Nancy. Both of these episodes, from *Oliver Twist*, are described in the pages that follow.

George Augustus Sala, an occasional walking companion of Dickens, noted how widely he was known:

> The omnibus conductors knew him, the street boys knew him … Elsewhere he would make his appearance in the oddest places and in the most inclement weather: in Ratcliff Highway, on Haverstock Hill, on Camberwell Green, in Gray's Inn Road, in the Wandsworth Road, at Hammersmith Broadway, in Norton Folgate and at Kensal New Town.

Henry James, born an American whose literary style was very different from that of Dickens, saw the capital of his adopted nation in less sentimental, but perhaps more flattering, terms:

> London is on the whole the most possible form of life. I take it as an artist and a bachelor; as one who has the

> passion of observation and whose business is the study of human life. It is the biggest aggregation of human life – the most complete compendium of the world.

Virginia Woolf, herself a resident of Bloomsbury, puts into words the pleasures of walking in London through her character Mrs Dalloway: 'I love walking in London. Really it is better than walking in the country.'

Anthony Trollope also places many scenes in the capital, especially in the Palliser novels where much of the action occurs in Parliament or in the Inns of Court. One of his most chilling passages occurs in *The Prime Minister*, when the crooked financier Ferdinand Lopez makes his final, despairing walk. Lopez has failed in a series of dishonest deals and further failed to extract money from the family of his unfortunate wife whom he married contrary to the wishes of her parents:

> [Lopez] went round by Trafalgar Square and along the Strand and up some dirty streets by the small theatres and so on to Holborn and by Bloomsbury Square up to Tottenham Court Road, then through some unused street into Portland Place, along the Marylebone Road and back to Manchester Square by Baker Street.

It is still possible to follow Lopez's route, after which he buys the single ticket to 'Tenways Junction' and commits suicide by throwing himself in front of a train.

This book is arranged by districts based on London's boroughs so that, for the most part, readers can follow their interests on foot. This works well in areas which are rich in literary associations such as Westminster, Mayfair, the City of London and Bloomsbury, but is more difficult in outlying areas like

Blackheath and Highgate, where a bicycle or public transport will be required for all but the most resolute pedestrians.

Some authors, such as Evelyn Waugh (1903–66) and P.G. Wodehouse (1881–1975), mostly confined their characters to a relatively small area and in such cases the main entry in the area concerned may include a few references to other areas which occasionally feature in the writer's works. Other writers, like Dickens, crop up everywhere. Dickens and his family lived in innumerable addresses in London and he made use of many of them in his novels as homes, workplaces or points of departure for his characters, while some of his most memorable scenes were placed just beyond the capital. In one case the author has allowed himself some licence to stray over the border into Kent for a particularly striking episode from Dickens.

The Inns of Court (Lincoln's Inn, Gray's Inn and The Middle and Inner Temple) have been given their own separate entry because their long and rich history has endowed them with many literary associations. Although they are in two London Boroughs, Camden and the City, they are close enough to one another to be explored on foot with minimum use of public transport. There are also separate entries for the River Thames and London Fog, with which we will begin.

1

LONDON FOG

The author can remember a time in the 1960s when tins of 'London Fog' were on sale to tourists, though one assumes that if the tins were ever opened their contents would immediately have dispersed. In fact, the word 'fog' as found in the works of Dickens and Conan Doyle was a misnomer and should have been 'smog', a term common in the 1950s to describe the impenetrable and often fatal combination of fog and smoke that, in 1952 as 'The Great Smog', killed 12,000 people in London alone from bronchial disease. It prompted the Clean Air Act of 1956, which restricted the use of polluting fuels and banned black smoke.

Yet in 1802 Wordsworth, in his ode 'Composed Upon Westminster Bridge', could write:

> Earth has not anything to show more fair:
> Dull would he be of soul who could pass by
> A sight so touching in its majesty.
> This City now doth like a garment wear
> The beauty of the morning: silent, bare,
> Ships, towers, domes, theatres and temples lie
> Open unto the fields, and to the sky,
> All bright and glittering in the smokeless air.

Never did sun more beautifully steep
In his first splendour valley, rock or hill;
Ne'er saw I, never felt, a calm so deep!
The river glideth at his own sweet will:
Dear God! The very houses seem asleep
And all that mighty heart is lying still!

Wordsworth is thought of as a poet of the Lake District's mountains and valleys, but was clearly moved by the city and its 'smokeless air'. However, by 1819, just seventeen years after Wordsworth's ode, his fellow poet Shelley was writing in the opening lines of his poem 'Peter Bell the Third' that:

Hell is a City much like London –
A Populous and Smoky City.

A third poet, Byron, wrote in 'Don Juan' (1823) that Juan, arriving in London, was struck by:

A mighty mass of brick and smoke and shipping,
Dirty and dusky but as wide as eye could reach.

Byron declares that the smoke is like a dunce's cap:

A huge dun cupola, like a foolscap crown
On a fool's head – and there is London town.

So what had happened to Wordsworth's 'smokeless air'?

In the decades after Wordsworth wrote his poem, London began the rapid expansion, in both population and industry, that turned it from a city of fewer than a million inhabitants to more than six million, making it by far the greatest metropolis the world had ever seen. Its naturally foggy winter climate, combined with the smoke of domestic coal fires, railways and factories, turned its winter atmosphere into a subject of wonder.

The French writer Hippolyte Taine wrote in 1872: 'no words can describe the fog in winter. There are days when, holding a man by the hand, one cannot see his face' and he referred his readers to the works of the recently deceased Dickens to gain some insight into the nature of London's atmosphere.

Dickens's most enduring images of London smog occur in *Bleak House*, where the thickness of the 'fog' reflects the impenetrable obscurities of the case in chancery of Jarndyce and Jarndyce, whose endless legal wranglings eventually absorb the value of the entire estate which was the subject of the lawsuit. Based on a real case which dragged on for twenty years, the first page of the book sets the scene:

> Fog everywhere. Fog up the river where it flows among green eyots and meadows; fog down the river where it rolls defiled among the tiers of shipping and the waterside pollutions of a great and dirty city ... Fog on the Essex marshes, Fog on the Kentish heights.

The frequent use of the capital 'F' almost suggests that Dickens considers the fog to be a character in its own right. He carries the fog into the heart of *Bleak House*, with its legal delays and obscurities: 'at the very heart of the fog sits the Lord High Chancellor in his High Court of Chancery.'

Of all his works *Bleak House* is the one in which Dickens most clearly shows his frustration with the English legal system, its waste and its delays. The central feature of the book is the case of Jarndyce and Jarndyce, which is concerned with the distribution of an estate through the court of Chancery. One of the intended beneficiaries, Ada, goes to live with her kind elderly relative John Jarndyce, accompanied by her friend Esther Summerson, supposedly an orphan. A separate but related plot concerns the marriage of Sir Leicester Dedlock and his beautiful wife Lady Dedlock who, unknown to Sir Leicester, had a daughter by her wastrel lover, Captain Hawdon, before

Sherlock Holmes' favourite restaurant, Simpson's-in-the-Strand. (Ewan Munro)

she met Sir Leicester. She believes that both Hawdon and the daughter are dead, but they are in fact both alive, the daughter being Esther Summerson. The rascally lawyer, Tulkinghorn, learns Lady Dedlock's secret and threatens to expose her, but is murdered by Lady Dedlock's maid Hortense, though not before Sir Leicester has learned of his wife's former affair. Lady Dedlock flees and perishes before her husband is able to tell her that he has forgiven her. The book is particularly rich in its cast of lesser characters, such as Mrs Jellyby whose chaotic philanthropy reduces her household to chaos.

Elsewhere in the book, Dickens has his character Mr Guppy explain to the innocent and angelic Esther Summerson (Dickens's only female narrator) the additional phenomenon of London's smoke. When she arrives in London, Esther comments: 'We drove slowly through the dirtiest and darkest streets that ever were seen in the world, I thought, and in such a distracting state of confusion that I wondered how the people kept their senses.' She asks Mr Guppy: 'whether there was a great fire anywhere? For the streets were so full of dense brown smoke that scarcely anything was to be seen.'

'Oh dear no miss,' he said. 'This is a London particular.'

The celebrated London restaurant Simpson's-in-the-Strand, where Sherlock Holmes and Dr Watson would dine, calls its thick pea soup 'London Particular' in tribute to Dickens's coining of the term, which has also found applications elsewhere in the names of societies and restaurants. Simpson's, famous for its particularly English dishes, makes a brief appearance in E.M. Forster's novel *Howard's End* when Margaret Schlegel is taken there by Henry Wilcox, whom she will later marry:

> 'What'll you have?'
> 'Fish pie', said she, with a glance at the menu.
> 'Fish pie! Fancy coming for fish pie to Simpson's.
> It's not a bit the thing to go for here … Saddle of mutton and cider to drink. That's the type of thing. I like this place for a joke, once in a way. It's so thoroughly Old English.'

Other authors make use of London's atmosphere in their stories. Robert Louis Stevenson's Jekyll and Hyde conduct their business through 'the swirling wreaths' of London fog, while in *The Sign of Four* Dr Watson and Sherlock Holmes take a cab to Lambeth in dense fog, where Watson writes that: '[I] soon lost my bearings … Sherlock Holmes was never at fault however and he muttered the names as the cab rattled through squares and in and out by tortuous by-streets.'

Elizabeth Barrett Browning, in her poem 'Aurora Leigh', wrote of London's fog wiping out London:

> I saw
> Fog only, the great tawny weltering fog,
> Involve the passive city, strangle it
> Alive, and draw it off into the void,
> Spires, bridges, streets and squares, as if a sponge
> Had wiped out London

Yet, not all references to London's fogs are critical. In 1937, as London's smogs approached their fatal peak, George Gershwin's song 'A Foggy Day in London Town' ends on an optimistic note:

> A foggy day in London Town
> Had me low and had me down
> I viewed the morning with alarm
> The British Museum had lost its charm.
> How long, I wondered, could this thing last?
> But the age of miracles hadn't passed,
> For, suddenly, I saw you there
> And through foggy London Town
> The sun was shining everywhere.

London's fogs are not what they were. Those of the twenty-first century are feeble imitations of the smoky atmosphere in which Sherlock Holmes and *Bleak House*'s blackmailing lawyer Tulkinghorn conducted their murky business but as long as the novels of Dickens and Conan Doyle are read the fogs will not be forgotten.

2

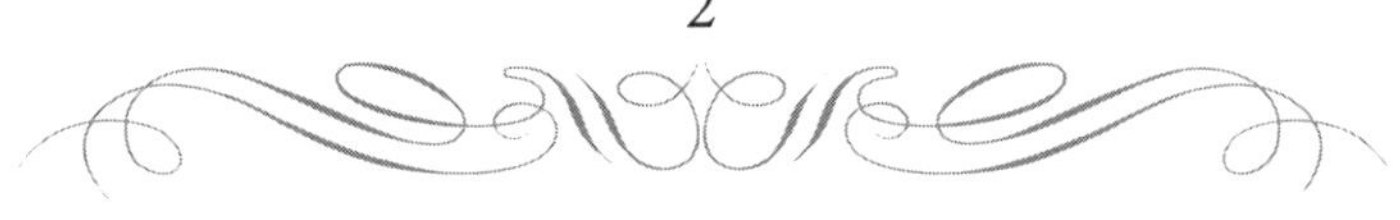

THE RIVER THAMES

In the middle of the nineteenth century, when London's sewage flowed into the Thames, it was a major transmitter of waterborne diseases such as typhoid, which infected Queen Victoria as a young woman; probably killed her husband Albert, the Prince Consort (the cause is not certain); and came close to killing her heir, the future Edward VII. Four cholera epidemics between 1831 and 1866 killed almost 40,000 citizens in London alone. It was not always thus. The Elizabethan poet Edmund Spenser (*c.*1552–99), a contemporary of Shakespeare, wrote a poem to celebrate the marriages of Kathleen and Elizabeth Somerset, the daughters of the Earl of Worcester, one of his patrons. Like many poets of the time (and since) he was endlessly in search of wealthy patrons to support him and in the first verse of the poem he refers to his 'long fruitlesse stay in Prince's Court' and of finding consolation in 'Sweete Thames'.

Calm was the day, and through the trembling ayre
Sweete breathing Zephyrus did softly play
A gentle spirit, that lightly did delay
Hot Titans beames, which then did glister fayre
When I (whom sullein care,

Through discontent of my long fruitlesse stay
In Princes Court, and expectation vayne
Of idle hopes, which still doe fly away,
Like empty shaddowes, did afflict my brayne)
Walkt forth to ease my payne
Along the shoare of silver streaming Themmes;
Whose rutty Bancke, the which his River hemmes,
Was paynted all with variable flowers,
And all the meads adornd with daintie gemmes
Fit to decke maydens bowres,
And crowne their Paramours
Against the Brydale day, which is not long:
Sweete themmes! runne softly, till I end my Song.

In the twentieth century, T.S. Eliot used Spenser's closing line as an opening to a rather more jaded comment on the river:

Sweet Thames, run softly till I end my song,
The river bears no empty bottles, sandwich papers;
Silk handkerchiefs, cardboard boxes, cigarette ends
Or other testimony of summer nights.

The drainage works of Sir Joseph Bazalgette (1819–91) helped cleanse the river of sewage, but did little to protect it from the detritus of twentieth-century consumer society with its need for packaging and cigarettes. Bazalgette's drainage works themselves became the centrepiece of a novel published in 2005. *The Great Stink* by Clare Clark (not to be confused with a work which bears the same title by the present author, and is an account of Bazalgette's life and work) tells the story of William May, a soldier of the Crimean War, who returns, traumatised by his experiences in that terrible conflict, and works with Bazalgette on the drainage systems which were being constructed in the 1850s and 1860s. William becomes a suspect when the body of a murdered man is discovered in the sewers and in the story the author incorporates a number of people and activities which were indeed involved in Bazalgette's great project. Joseph Bazalgette himself (not yet Sir Joseph, which came in 1875) is asked what makes a good engineer and replies: 'a pragmatist made conservative by the conspicuous failures of structures and machines hastily contrived.' William is eventually exonerated and the book concludes with the execution, at Newgate, of the real culprit.

A more tragic note was sounded by Andrew Motion, in his poem 'Fresh Water', written in memory of Ruth Haddon, a young woman who drowned with fifty others on 20 August 1989 following a collision near Cannon Street railway bridge between the dredger *Bowbelle* and the pleasure boat *Marchioness*, on which a party was being held:

> Afterwards we lean on the railings outside a café. It's
> autumn.
> The water is speckled with leaves, and a complicated
> tangle of junk
> Bumps against the Embankment wall: a hank of bright
> grass,
> A rotten bulrush stem, a fragment of dark polished
> wood.
> One of the children asks if people drown in the river, and
> I think
> Of Ruth, who was on the Marchioness. After her death,
> I met
> someone who had survived.

Finally, the contemporary poet Jeremy Hooker (born 1941) in 'City Walking, 1', visited St Mary's Church, Battersea, where William Blake (1757–1827) was married and from which Turner had painted the river. He sees the river from which:

Turner
Sat to paint clouds
And sunsets over the water –
Where we can see tower blocks,
Luxury flats, a marina,
A power station,
That drives the Underground

The power station referred to was at Lots Road, Chelsea and was constructed from 1902–05, much to the indignation of the American-born artist James McNeil Whistler (1834–1903) who was offended by its monstrous size and would no doubt have been appalled to see his words applied to a Second World War poster entitled 'The Proud City'. It depicted the distinctive outline of the power station against a background of searchlights and bore Whistler's own words:

> The poor buildings lose themselves in the dim sky and the tall chimneys become campanili and the warehouses are palaces in the night and the whole city hangs in the heavens.

Lots Road ceased to provide power for the Underground in 2002 and the site is at present being redeveloped into shops, offices and luxury flats.

3

THE CITY OF LONDON

Despite its role as a centre of commerce, the City of London has many literary associations, not least because it has been around for much longer than most of the rest of London. Indeed, some parts of it could accommodate a book of literary associations on their own. Given the number and variety of such connections, it is not easy to present them in a form which will suit all readers. Broadly, the chapter begins at the eastern end of the City and moves west towards Fleet Street, though with many diversions to accommodate the City's rich history and to suit the whims of such personalities as Oliver Twist and Samuel Pickwick.

The 'Square Mile' of the City itself owes its identity to the Roman wall built to surround their settlement of 'Londinium'. Portions of the wall may still be seen, notably those close to the Tower of London and a substantial section found in the Barbican, near the church of St Giles, Cripplegate, in Fore Street.

St Giles, Cripplegate, is one of London's most interesting churches, with strong literary connections. The poet John Milton is buried in this attractive little church, which was restored after being bombed during the Second World War. It also contains the tomb of John Foxe, author of *Foxe's Book of Martyrs*, and it was the church where Oliver Cromwell was married and the children of Edmund Shakespeare were baptised. Edmund's brother William is believed to have stood as their godfather, a tradition fortified by the discovery in 2007 that William was lodging nearby. The church also holds the tomb of Sir Thomas Lucy, lampooned in *The Merry Wives of Windsor* as Justice Shallow after the young William was involved in a poaching incident in Lucy's deer park near Shakespeare's Stratford home.

GRUB STREET

Running north from the Barbican towards Moorfields, in the vicinity of St Giles, is Milton Street, which until 1830 was called Grub Street, described by Samuel Johnson in his *Dictionary* as 'much inhabited by writers of small histories, dictionaries and temporary poems, whence any mean production is called grubstreet.' Johnson himself worked there for a while and from 1730 to 1737 the *Grub Street Journal*, a satirical magazine, took its name from the street and targeted members of the literary establishment. During the eighteenth century, Grub Street was the home of several journals which were regarded as scurrilous by the authorities. Many of the publishers were prosecuted, including the publisher of John Wilkes's journal the *North Briton*.

John Wilkes (1725–97) was born in Clerkenwell, became MP for Aylesbury in 1757 and in 1762 launched a paper called the *North Briton* which attacked the government of George III, led by Lord Bute. Wilkes was prosecuted for seditious libel, but the charge was dismissed by the Lord Chief Justice on the grounds that Wilkes was an MP. When Parliament amended the relevant law, Wilkes fled to Paris and returned in 1768 to stand as MP for Middlesex. A farcical series of events led to Wilkes's repeated election, expulsion from Parliament, arrest, imprisonment, fine and riots in Wilkes's favour. He campaigned

St Giles, Cripplegate, has strong literary connections. (Ewan Munro)

for freedom of the press, Parliamentary reform and supported the rebellious American colonies in their opposition to the government. In 1774 he became Lord Mayor of London. Informed by his former friend and one-time supporter, the Earl of Sandwich, that he would die on the gallows or of the pox, he replied: 'That, my lord, will depend upon whether I embrace your principles or your mistress.'

In 1728 Alexander Pope lampooned Grub Street in his satirical poem 'The Dunciad', which is a thinly veiled attack on anyone, especially fellow writers, who had offended the thin-skinned poet. One of his targets was John Dryden, who was satirised along with other members of 'the Grub Street race' who wrote primarily for money. Dr Samuel Johnson, himself a Grub Street writer, would have been unmoved by Pope's criticism since Johnson himself averred that 'no man but a blockhead ever wrote except for money'.

The expression 'Grub Street' was soon taken to mean any low-quality hack writing, or the struggling writers who produced it, and this usage is reflected in George Gissing's novel of 1891, *New Grub Street*. It features Edwin Rearden, a novelist of some talent and high ideals, who struggles to earn a living; and the cynical and calculating Jasper Milvain, who willingly undertakes hack writing for money while despising those who publish and read his work. Edwin dies and Jasper prospers.

Aldersgate Street, nearby, and the gate from which it took its name, is recalled by Dickens in *The Adventures of Martin Chuzzlewit*, the site of the Chuzzlewits's warehouse being Aldersgate Street. And it is close to Aldersgate, in Saxe-Coburg Square (a site north of Cowcross Street, in fact Albion Place), that Sherlock Holmes takes Dr Watson in his search for the scene of a crime in *The Red-headed League*.

The Adventures of Martin Chuzzlewit was published in 1844. Martin is the grandson of old Martin, a wealthy gentleman who resents the demands made on him by his spendthrift family and has adopted Mary Graham, a young orphan, whom he treats as his daughter. Young Martin leaves his grandfather in the care of the dishonest architect Pecksniff, whose true character and desire to share the Chuzzlewit wealth gradually become evident. Young Martin, who has been disinherited by his grandfather for falling in love with Mary, goes to America with his friend Mark Tapley where they both fall ill with malaria, are swindled by American fraudsters in a land deal and lose their modest fortunes (an episode which caused considerable offence to Dickens's many American readers). Wiser and less selfish, young Martin returns to England and uncovers Pecksniff's treachery. His grandfather recognises that he is a reformed character and allows him to marry Mary. A separate plot concerns Jonas Chuzzlewit, nephew to old Martin and cousin to young Martin, a brutal husband and murderer who later commits suicide, and the novel also includes one of Dickens's most memorable minor characters, Mrs Gamp, the gin-swilling, umbrella-carrying midwife.

LONDON'S GATES

Cripplegate and Aldersgate are two of the Roman and medieval gates through which travellers were admitted to the city during hours of daylight and which enable us to trace the route of the Roman wall itself. From Moorgate, in the north, the gates run clockwise through Bishopsgate, Aldgate, Billingsgate, Dowgate, Ludgate, Newgate, St John's Gate, Aldersgate and Cripplegate. Some of the gates themselves have literary connections. The twelfth-century St John's Gate, for example, north of Smithfield, which was extensively refurbished in 2010, was for a time the home of the artist William Hogarth and of the *Gentleman's Magazine* which employed Dr Samuel Johnson, Oliver Goldsmith and the actor David Garrick. The gate now contains a small museum.

St Botolph, Bishopsgate, is the scene of one of John Betjeman's sadder poems, heavy with nostalgia as he thinks of his family. The poem, simply entitled 'City', tells how, amidst the odour of incense:

> I sit down
> In St Botolph Bishopsgate churchyard
> And wait for the spirit of my grandfather
> Toddling along from the Barbican

The grandfather referred to had hoped that John would continue to run the family business, based in the Pentonville Road, making fine furniture, but the future poet had no interest, despite the pleas of his father in 'Summoned by Bells':

Well now, my boy, I want your solemn word
To carry on the firm when I am gone
Fourth generation John, they look to you.
I was a poet. That was why I failed.

Bishopsgate is close to the site of another location with strong literary associations – Crosby Square, formerly Crosby Place. This was the original site of Crosby Hall, built in 1475 for a wealthy grocer, Sir John Crosby. In 1483 it became the home of Richard, Duke of Gloucester, later Richard III, who had the great misfortune to have his character blackened by William Shakespeare, ably assisted by Sir Laurence Olivier in the film of that name. When ordering his henchmen to execute his brother, the hapless Duke of Clarence, to clear his route to the throne, Richard instructs them:

When you have done repair to Crosby Place,
But sirs, be sudden in the execution,
Withal obdurate, do not hear him plead;
For Clarence is well-spoken and perhaps
May move your hearts to pity if you mark him.

Clarence is duly drowned in a barrel of Malmsey wine and Richard proceeds on his murderous way until final defeat at Bosworth at the hands of Henry VII.

In 1532 Crosby Hall became the home of Sir Thomas More, author of *Utopia*, a fictional account of an ideal state. In 1908 the site was bought by a bank and Crosby Hall was moved lock, stock and barrel to Danvers Street, Chelsea, close to the Thames and to the site of Sir Thomas More's Chelsea home, where it is now the home of a wealthy businessman (see Chapter 7).

Crosby Square also appears in Conan Doyle's story *The Man with the Twisted Lip*, first published in the *Strand Magazine* in 1891 and considered by the author to be one of his best

Sherlock Holmes stories: a tale of opium dens and elaborate disguises. Neville St Clair, a Kentish gentleman, works in the City but has lodgings in 'Upper Swandam Lane', east of London Bridge, whence he issues as a cripple called Hugh Boone, a Threadneedle Street match-seller with a 'shock of orange hair, a pale face disfigured by a horrible scar'. The story resembled the real life of Cecil Brown Smith from Norwood, who posed as a paralysed match-seller in Bishopsgate before being seen to exit Crosby Square as a fit young man. Smith was later sentenced to hard labour, having also posed as a clergyman and performed illegal marriage ceremonies.

Aldgate, the gatehouse itself, was the home of Geoffrey Chaucer when he was employed as a collector of Customs in the reign of Richard II, and in 1381, from within its walls, Chaucer witnessed the arrival of the Essex insurgents of the Peasants' Revolt, led by Jack Straw. He would have seen them pass through the gate on their way to their fatal encounter with Richard II at Smithfield, where their leader, Wat Tyler, was stabbed by the Lord Mayor of London and the rebellion was ended.

Baroness Orczy (1865–1947), a Hungarian aristocrat more prosaically known as Mrs Montague Barstow, made Aldgate tube station a central feature of her detective story *The Mysterious Death on the Underground Railway*, in which a young woman is found dead in a carriage at Aldgate station. The story depends upon the fact that in the year of its publication, 1901, the Metropolitan Railway had lost passengers to the Central London Railway (now the Central Line) and that the empty carriages of the Metropolitan made it a suitable place to carry out a murder.

Dickens also refers to coaching inns near Aldgate. Samuel Pickwick sets out for Ipswich by coach from the Bull at Aldgate (now in Devonshire Row, Aldgate) and David Copperfield arrives at the nearby Blue Boar (formerly at No. 30 High Street, Aldgate) to enter Salem House School to which he has been sent by his cruel stepfather, Murdstone. He is miserable at Salem House under the tyrannical rule of its head, the flogger Creakle, his only consolation being his friendship with Steerforth, a ruthless charmer who goes on to wreck the lives of David's friends the Peggottys. The Salem House connection also leads to David's entry into Murdstone's warehouse (mirroring Dickens's spell in a blacking factory) and also his introduction to Wilkins Micawber, David's generous but improvident landlord and one of Dickens's most memorable characters. Micawber is an affectionate portrait of the novelist's well-meaning but hopelessly improvident father, John Dickens, whose inability to manage money earned him a spell in the Marshalsea Prison for debtors. Micawber's financial improvidence is such that he often has to move home, one of his many homes being in Windsor Terrace just north of the City Road. Windsor Terrace boasts a fine block of flats called Micawber Court, which would have been far beyond the means of their namesake. The City features in many other parts of Dickens's novels, the home of Anthony and Jonas Chuzzlewit being at 5 Foster Lane, near St Paul's and close to Wood Street, at whose Cross Keys Inn Pip, in *Great Expectations*, arrives by coach with Estella.

David Copperfield was published in 1850 and Dickens declared 'Of all my books I like this the best'. It has a strong autobiographical element. Brought up by his widowed mother and a cruel stepfather, David is sent, after his mother's early death, to the hateful Salem House School where, despite the tyrannical headmaster, he makes two friends: the attractive but selfish Steerforth and the steadfast and honest Traddles. Sent into menial employment (like Dickens at the blacking factory), he meets Wilkins Micawber whose inability to manage money is a recurring theme of his life. Desperate to escape his wretched life, David walks to the home of his aunt, Betsey Trotwood, being robbed on the way. Kindly received by her, he is articled to a firm of solicitors, Spenlow and Jorkins, in Doctors' Commons, falling in love with the pretty but brainless Dora, Spenlow's daughter. Re-acquainted with Steerforth, David introduces him to the family of his old nurse Clara Peggotty, her husband a Yarmouth fisherman, and to a cousin of the family, Little Em'ly. Steerforth seduces Little Em'ly, runs away with her, but then abandons her, causing much distress and a long search by the Peggottys to recover her. Steerforth is drowned and David marries the empty-headed Dora Spenlow before becoming famous as an author. Dora, a cruel caricature of the author's loving but neglected wife Catherine, dies and David marries again, his wife this time being the level-headed Agnes whom he has long known and come late to appreciate. Agnes's father has become the victim of the machinations of a villainous clerk, Uriah Heep, who is finally exposed by Wilkins Micawber and Traddles. Uriah Heep is jailed and Micawber (for whom always 'something will turn up') emigrates to a new life in Australia.

CORNHILL, LOMBARD STREET & CANNON STREET

Many of the City's streets bear ancient names. One of the earliest English poems, 'Piers Plowman' by William Langland (*c.* 1330–86), a poem written in about 1370, makes many references to London, such as 'Thus he awaked, woet good, whan he wonede in Cornehull [Cornhill]' and there are five references to Lombard Street, including 'I lerned among Lumbardes a lesson and of Jewes'. This is a reference to the fact that, in the fourteenth century, usury (lending money for interest) was forbidden by the Church and the only groups who were able to lend money were Jews. However, the Lombards, from the area around Milan in northern Italy, had managed to evade this prohibition by a form of pawnbroking. A security would be given by a borrower in exchange for a loan and the security would be redeemed for more than the value of the original loan: a disguised interest payment. Lombard Street, in the heart of the City, remains at the heart of banking and is the home of many financial institutions. It is no surprise, therefore, that Dickens chose nearby Cornhill as the site of Scrooge's counting house to which Bob Cratchit walked each day in *A Christmas Carol*.

The Green Dragon at 3 Bull's Head Passage, Leadenhall market, close to Cornhill, was where Pickwick's faithful and memorable valet, Sam Weller, wrote a Valentine to Mary who eventually became his wife. Bull's Head Passage is now well supplied with restaurants and wine bars for the City folk who work nearby, though the Green Dragon is no more.

In Baroness Orczy's (1865–1947) crime thriller *Lady Molly of Scotland Yard* the murder victim had his office in Lombard Street, while Wilkie Collins's *Moonstone* was pledged to a banker there.

A play of 1598 called *The First and Second Parte of Edward the IV*, whose author is unknown, gives an account of the rebellion of Jack Cade in 1450, making reference to many City streets whose names are still in use today as the rebels made their way along Leadenhall, Lombard Street and Cheapside in their quest for blood and plunder. However, Jack Cade, who claims Plantagenet descent and calls himself John Mortimer, first lays claim to London by striking the London Stone in Shakespeare's *Henry VI Part II*.

> Now is Mortimer lord of this city. And here, sitting
> upon London-stone, I charge and command that, of the
> city's cost, the pissing-conduit run nothing but
> claret wine this first year of our reign. And now
> henceforward it shall be treason for any that calls
> me other than Lord Mortimer.

The London Stone, a strange relic of London's ancient history, now lies embedded behind an iron grill in the wall of No. 111 Cannon Street, which until recently formed the premises of a Chinese bank. It will shortly be moved to a more dignified site at the Walbrook Building on the corner of Cannon Street and Walbrook. It is also known as the Brutus Stone, having supposedly been brought to London by a Trojan prince called Brutus following the fall of Troy. His followers, known as Brutons, gave their name to their new home (i.e. Britain) and founded New Troy which, during the reign of one of Brutus's successors, King Lud, became known as Lud's Town or London. By the time of the Norman Conquest the stone had given its name to the area surrounding it, where it was marked on maps as Londonstane, and the first Mayor of London, who took office in 1192, was called Henry Fitzailwyn de Londonstane. It is likely that it was used by the Romans as a point from which to measure distances to other Roman settlements and the poet William Blake identified it as an object where Druids carried out ritual sacrifices. It has also been advanced as a candidate for the stone from which King Arthur drew the sword Excalibur in Malory's *Le Morte d'Arthur*. The stone was moved to its present position when Wren's church of St Swithin's, which previously accommodated it, was destroyed by bombing in 1941 and an ancient legend claims that 'So long as the Stone of Brutus is safe, so long shall London flourish'.

In about 1390 an anonymous Kentish poet wrote a scathing account of London in *London Lickpenny*, which presents the experience of an innocent countryman faced with the cynicism and corruption of traders, lawyers and other denizens of the metropolis. He, too, makes reference to the London Stone in Canywike (Cannon) Street with its population of drapers and candlemakers, after whom the street was originally named:

> Then went I forth by London Stone
> Throughout all Canywike Street,
> Drapers to me they called anon
> Great chepe of cloth they gan me hete [offer]

But the verse, like all verses, ends 'but for lack of money I might not spend'.

William Blake, in his lengthy work 'Jerusalem', written between 1804 and 1820, penned and illustrated a vision of London which contrasts the heavenly and earthly cities, the latter including reference to supposed sacrifices by Druids. It begins with a flattering description of familiar parts of London:

> The fields from Islington to Marylebone
> To Primrose Hill and saint John's Wood,
> Were builded over with pillars of gold,
> And there Jerusalem's pillars stood.

But it goes on to describe how 'The Druids' golden Knife' revelled in human gore whose victims:

> Groaned aloud on London Stone
> They groaned aloud on Tyburn's Brook,
> Albion gave his deadly groan,
> And all the Atlantic mountains shook.

The stone itself, which is at present unnoticed by all but the most observant pedestrians in Cannon Street, is a Grade II listed monument.

CHEAPSIDE

In his *Cook's Tale* Chaucer makes reference to the disorderly behaviour of Cheapside apprentices, one of whom is singled out:

> At every wedding he would sing and hop
> And he preferred the tavern to the shop.
> Whenever any pageant or procession

Came down Cheapside, goodbye to his profession.
He'd leap out of the shop to see the sight
And join the dance and not come back that night!

Wood Street, off Cheapside, was celebrated by William Wordsworth in his poem 'The Reverie of Poor Susan', in which the poet also makes reference to two other familiar City streets:

At the corner of Wood Street, when daylight appears,
Hangs a Thrush that sings loud, it has sung for three
years:
Poor Susan has pass'd by the spot, and has heard
In the silence of morning the song of the bird.
'Tis a note of enchantment: what ails her? She sees
A mountain ascending, a vision of trees;
Bright volumes of vapour through Lothbury glide,
And a river flows on through the vale of Cheapside.

The tree, a plane tree, survives in the churchyard of St Peter Westcheap, Wood Street. The tree, ancient and gnarled, and surrounded by a small shrubbery, is a rare sight in this part of the City and a notice reminds the passer-by that it was the subject of Wordsworth's poem.

Even before the time of Wordsworth the noise and energy of the City were making a strong impression on visitors. In his final and finest work *The Expedition of Humphry Clinker*, Tobias Smollett (1721–71) recorded the impressions of someone who was unfamiliar with the metropolis:

I start every hour from my sleep, at the horrid noise of the watchmen bawling the hour through every street and thundering at every door. In the morning I start out of bed, in consequence of the still more dreadful alarm made by the country carts and noisy rustics bellowing 'green peas' under my window … All is tumult and

> hurry; one would imagine they were impelled by some disorder of the brain that will not suffer them to be at rest … possessed by a spirit more absurd and pernicious than anything we meet within the precincts of Bedlam [which at that time was located in Bishopsgate].

QUEEN VICTORIA STREET

Running parallel to Cheapside, Queen Victoria Street was constructed in the 1860s to link the Bank of England, at its east end, with the Victoria Embankment, which was opened in 1870 to provide a route from the heart of the City to Parliament. On the north side of Queen Victoria Street, on the Faraday Building, is a plaque which marks the fact that this was the last home of Doctors' Commons, a college of law (in effect an Inn of Court) which at one time numbered Sir Thomas More amongst its members. Originally based in Paternoster Row near St Paul's Cathedral, it moved to what is now Queen Victoria Street where Dickens rented an office for a time.

By Dickens's time, Doctors' Commons was in terminal decline. In *David Copperfield* David became an articled clerk with Spenlow and Jorkins at Doctors' Commons, which is described in the book as 'a cosy, dosy, old fashioned, time-forgotten sleepy-headed little family party'. It was dissolved in 1865, its members moving to other Inns of Court, and its premises were demolished in 1867 to make way for Queen Victoria Street. While at Spenlow and Jorkins, David received from Francis Spenlow, his future father-in-law, some advice about 'the best sort of professional business' which reflected Dickens's jaundiced view of the legal profession and which underpinned the legal obfuscations of Jarndyce and Jarndyce in *Bleak House*. Spenlow tells David that the best business is:

> … a good case of a disputed will where there was a neat little estate of thirty or forty thousand pounds was perhaps the best of all. In such a case, he said, not only were there very pretty pickings in the way of arguments at every stage of the proceedings … but, the costs being pretty sure to come out of the proceeds of the estate at last, both sides went at it in a lively and spirited manner and expense was no consideration.

LONDON BRIDGE

T.S. Eliot worked in the Foreign and Colonial Department of Lloyd's bank behind St Mary Woolnoth, near Bank station in the heart of the City. In 'The Waste Land' Eliot recorded his impressions as he made his way across London Bridge with other commuters on their way to what Eliot regarded as dull city jobs:

> Unreal city,
> Under the brown fog of a winter dawn,
> A crowd flowed over London Bridge, so many,
> I had not thought death had undone so many.
> Sighs, short and infrequent, were exhaled,
> And each man fixed his eyes before his feet.
> Flowed up the hill and down King William Street,
> To where Saint Mary Woolnoth kept the hours
> With a dead sound on the final stroke of nine.

Dickens, too, makes many references to London Bridge and placed a number of his more alarming episodes in its vicinity. David Copperfield, in flight from the cruelty of Creakle at Salem House, begins his long walk to Dover and to the safe arms of his aunt, Betsey Trotwood, from here. The steps on the Surrey bank of the Thames, leading down from London

Bridge are also the scene of Nancy's conversation with Rose Maylie which ultimately leads to her death in *Oliver Twist.*

Oliver Twist, published in 1838, was Dickens's second novel, and tells the story of Oliver, an orphan of unknown parentage brought up in harsh conditions in a workhouse from which he flees. In fact, Oliver is heir to a share in the estate of his late father, a fact of which he is unaware. Oliver's half-brother, Monks, pays a gang of thieves led by Fagin and the violent Bill Sikes to lead Oliver into a life of crime which will thereby exclude him from his father's inheritance, leaving it all to Monks. Oliver resists all attempts to turn him into a criminal and is taken under the wing of the benevolent Mr Brownlow, but the gang abduct him from Mr Brownlow's care and he is sent on a burglary expedition with Bill Sikes, during which Oliver is injured and taken into the household of Rose and her guardian, the kind Mrs Maylie. Bill Sikes's companion, Nancy, learns of the plot to corrupt Oliver and reveals it to Rose, but the conversation is overheard by a member of the gang, Noah Claypole, and Sikes, enraged, beats Nancy to death, after which he flees and dies, accidentally hanging himself near Jacob's Island while escaping from an angry mob. Fagin is executed, Oliver learns of his fortune and is adopted by Mr Brownlow, and Rose turns out to be his mother's lost sister, his aunt.

The present London Bridge was built in the 1960s and the steps on which Nancy sat were removed, together with the bridge Dickens knew, to Lake Havasu City in Arizona.

The north bank of the river Thames, close to the bridge, is chosen by Jonas Chuzzlewit as the place to which he commits bloodstained clothing after murdering Tigg. Just to the north of London Bridge is the Todgers's boarding house in the same novel, *The Adventures of Martin Chuzzlewit*, in the labyrinth of streets that surround the Monument to the Great Fire of 1666. One of these, running east towards the Tower of London, is Eastcheap where, in *Henry IV Part II*, Shakespeare placed the

Boar's Head tavern, presided over by Mistress Quickly and a haunt of Falstaff and his friends. Rebuilt after the Great Fire it stood close to the present junction with Gracechurch Street and was finally demolished in 1831 to make way for King William IV Street.

Lower Thames Street, on the north side of London Bridge, accommodates the wharf to which Pip in *Great Expectations* takes a boat as part of his plan to remove the fugitive Magwitch from England. The meeting of Pip and Magwitch takes place in the churchyard of St James, Cooling, on the Isle of Grain in the North Kent marshes where Pip is confronted by Magwitch, demanding food, while visiting the grave of his parents and brothers. Pip thereby earns the gratitude of Magwitch who becomes his benefactor.

Great Expectations was published in 1861 and is often associated with the memorable film of the book made by David Lean in 1946. Pip, an orphan, who lives with his shrewish sister and her kindly blacksmith husband Joe Gargery, befriends a fleeing convict called Magwitch and is later introduced to Miss Havisham, a woman abandoned on her wedding day who remains in her wedding dress, surrounded by wedding paraphernalia, in a darkened room. In Berners Street, which runs north from Oxford Street, Dickens recorded that he encountered an eccentric woman clad all in white – the model for Miss Havisham. Miss Havisham has adopted a girl, Estella, whom she has groomed to be vain and contemptuous of men. During his visits to Miss Havisham Pip falls in love with the cold and moody Estella. Pip receives money from a mysterious benefactor (whom he assumes to be Miss Havisham) and goes to London to become a gentleman (and hence more worthy of Estella), meeting in the process Herbert Pocket, the lawyer Jaggers and his clerk Wemmick. Pip learns that his real benefactor is the convict Magwitch who, after being transported to Australia, made a fortune, but Pip, in his new life as a gentleman, distances himself from Magwitch and the kindly Joe Gargery who brought him up. Estella, who, it turns out, is Magwitch's long-lost daughter, marries a cruel husband, Bentley Drummle, and Magwitch, who has illegally returned from transportation, will be executed if he is caught. Pip tries to arrange Magwitch's escape from England, but Magwitch is caught as the result of a former partner in crime called Compeyson, who drowns and is revealed as the man who deserted Miss Havisham on her wedding day. Magwitch escapes execution by dying of injuries and Pip marries Estella whose husband has died.

In *Nicholas Nickleby* the mean-spirited Ralph Nickleby chooses 'Spigwiffin's Wharf' as the site for the run-down home of his niece Kate and her mother. Dickens places it near London Bridge in Lower Thames Street, now populated by offices. He doesn't make it sound very attractive:

> … a large old dingy house in Thames Street, the door and windows of which were so bespattered with mud that it would have appeared to be uninhabited for years … Old and gloomy and black in truth it was, and sullen and dark were the rooms once so bustling with life and enterprise … no life was stirring there. It was a picture of cold, silent decay.

Nicholas Nickleby was published in instalments in 1838–39 and is the story of Nicholas, 19, whose father has died. He is sent by his hostile uncle Ralph Nickleby, a wealthy businessman, to work at Dotheboys Hall, a horrible school run by the sadistic Wackford Squeers, who is particularly cruel to Smike, a simple-minded lad he uses as a drudge. Nicholas's mother and sister Kate are accommodated in dreary lodgings in a London slum owned by Ralph. Nicholas thrashes Squeers and flees with Smike and after many adventures, including a spell with some travelling players, Nicholas is offered employment by the benevolent and warm-hearted Cheeryble brothers, London merchants, whose generous attitude to the world contrasts with that of Ralph Nickleby. The Cheerybles also provide Nicholas's family with a home. Ralph, frustrated by Nicholas's success in creating a pleasant life for himself, attempts to remove Smike from Nicholas's care. He fails, but Smike dies of consumption and Ralph, learning that Smike was in fact his son, hangs himself in despair. Nicholas marries Madeline Bray, whom Ralph had intended for another; Nicholas's sister Kate marries the Cheerybles's nephew Frank; and Wackford Squeers is sentenced to transportation.

At that time, of course, (now Lower) Thames Street would have backed onto the old, decaying wharves of the Port of London (soon to be swept away for the Victoria Embankment). But Dickens did his best to give the City a happier face in the same novel by creating 'City Square' in the vicinity of the offices of the saintly Cheeryble brothers between Threadneedle Street and Bishopsgate:

> The City Square has no enclosure save the lamp post in the middle and no grass but the weeds which spring up round its base. It is a quiet, little-frequented retired spot favourable to melancholy and contemplation … It is so quiet you can almost hear the ticking of your own watch when you stop to cool in its refreshing atmosphere.

Dickens uses the quiet little square to emphasise the difference between the honest and friendly Cheeryble brothers and the mean and scheming Ralph Nickleby with his grand office in the West End. Dickens's City Square was a product of the novelist's imagination, but just such a setting exists close to the Guildhall Library in Aldermanbury: a small garden dedicated to the memory of John Heming and Henry Condell, friends of William Shakespeare who, in 1623, prepared an edition of thirty-six of his plays in the famous *First Folio*, which also contained a likeness of the playwright. Without their enterprise many of the plays would have been lost forever.

GOSWELL ROAD, CASTLE COURT & CHANGE ALLEY

Many of Samuel Pickwick's misadventures occur within the City. He lodges with Mrs Bardell in Goswell Road (then called Goswell Street) and although his adventures take him to many places he is a Cockney at heart. In Pickwick's own words: 'As well might I be content to gaze on Goswell Street for ever without one effort to penetrate to the hidden counties which on every side surround it.' His bachelor apartment is described in some detail:

> Mr Pickwick's apartments in Goswell street, although on a limited scale, were not only of a very neat and comfortable description, but peculiarly adapted for the residence of a man of his genius and observation. His sitting-room was the first floor front, his bedroom the second floor front; and thus whether he were sitting at his desk in the parlour, or standing before the dressing-glass in his dormitory, he had an equal opportunity of contemplating human nature in all the phases it exhibits in that popular thoroughfare.

Goswell Road is now the home of the Society of Genealogists, a learned society devoted to research which would surely have been a haunt of Samuel Pickwick had he had the opportunity.

The Pickwick Papers or *The Posthumous Papers of the Pickwick Club*, published in instalments in 1836–37, was Dickens's first novel and is an account of the travels and adventures around England of Samuel Pickwick and his friends. It is not so much a story as a series of incidents: a Parliamentary election, an elopement, a breach of promise case brought against Pickwick himself, and other humorous incidents. Pickwick himself is a Cockney and his faithful servant, Sam Weller, is one of Dickens's most memorable characters.

Pickwick was much given to frequenting taverns in the City, one of his favourite haunts being the George and Vulture in Castle Court, off Lombard Street. It is mentioned many times and occupies a site which has accommodated an inn since the thirteenth century. Many proposals have been advanced to demolish it and develop its extremely valuable site, but on each occasion resolute campaigns have been launched to preserve it, most notably by Cedric Charles Dickens (1916–2006), the author's great-grandson. It is now the home of the Dickens Pickwick Club, who dine on Pickwick Pie (better known as steak and kidney pudding) in a room where Dickens himself dined shortly before he began to write *The Pickwick Papers*. The rather shabby, tobacco-stained Dickens Room looks as if it has not been redecorated since the time of Dickens but, nevertheless, hosts the celebrations of City bankers for Christmas lunches and similar occasions.

It is from Garraway's Coffee House in Change Alley, off Lombard Street, that Pickwick writes to his landlady to tell her what he wants for dinner. Garraway's, one of the oldest coffee houses in the City, was much frequented by Charles Dickens. It was demolished in 1874 but its former location is marked by a plaque in Change Alley which commemorates its predecessor, Jonathan's Coffee House which, from 1680 to 1778, served as London's Stock Exchange. Pickwick's briefest letter, 'Dear Mrs. B, chops and tomato sauce, Yours Pickwick', is later produced as evidence of the fact that he broke a promise to marry her, the trial taking place at the Court of Common Pleas in the Guildhall. Pickwick's conviction and his steadfast refusal to pay the £750 damages (then a substantial sum) to the disappointed lady leads to his confinement in the Fleet Prison for debtors, where he is soon joined by his faithful servant Sam

Weller. Their release is secured when Pickwick agrees to pay Mrs Bardell's costs, incurred by the rascally lawyers Dodson and Fogg. Their offices in Cornhill occupied the present site of the Royal Exchange. The Fleet Prison had been built in the twelfth century and was demolished in the 1840s to make way for the London, Chatham and Dover Railway, whose successors still use the Thameslink route which joins railways north and south of the Thames. The prison, London's most notorious prison for debtors, is remembered in Old Fleet Lane, close to its former site. Samuel Pickwick's view of the prison was unforgiving: 'I have seen enough … My head aches with these scenes and my heart too.'

FLEET STREET

Until new printing technology and new management brought about changes in the 1980s, Fleet Street and its adjoining streets were synonymous with the national press. Fetter Lane, which runs north from Fleet Street towards Holborn Circus, was the home of the *People's Banner* and its scheming and muck-raking editor Quintus Slide, who pursues Phineas Finn and others in Trollope's Palliser novels. The origin of the street's name is unclear but may well derive from an old French word *faitor*, meaning an idle and disreputable lawyer. The word was used by Chaucer to refer to beggars and imposters who haunted the street in the fourteenth century.

The former Daily Express Building in Fleet Street, black glass without and art deco within, may with confidence be identified as the headquarters of the *Daily Beast* in Evelyn Waugh's *Scoop*, which he subtitled 'a novel about journalists' and which ruthlessly and hilariously satirised the activities of popular newspapers. The building appeared many times in *Private Eye* as 'The Black Lubyanka', a reference to the infamous KGB headquarters in Moscow.

The George and Vulture in Castle Court, off Lombard Street, was a favourite haunt of Samuel Pickwick. (Jim Linwood)

Described at the time as 'Britain's most modern building for Britain's most modern newspaper', with the degree of modesty associated with its proprietor, Lord Beaverbrook, the Daily Express Building opened in 1932, shortly after Evelyn Waugh made a short and unsuccessful attempt to take up a career in journalism in its pages. The bullying proprietor of the *Daily Beast*, 'Lord Copper', combines confidence with sublime ignorance as he briefs the hapless William Boot on his forthcoming assignment in a remote African kingdom where war is confidently expected and eagerly anticipated by newspaper proprietors like Lord Copper. William is accustomed to writing a weekly column called 'Lush Places' on rural matters from the safety of Boot Magna Hall in an unidentified but remote part of the countryside where he feels at home. Through a case of mistaken identity he is summoned to the headquarters of the *Daily Beast* at Nos 700–853 Fleet Street (in reality Nos 121–128), where Lord Copper sits behind 'massive double doors which by their weight, polish and depravity of design, proclaimed unmistakeably "Nothing but Us stands between you and Lord Copper"'.

Copper advises William to take with him a supply of cleft sticks for carrying messages through the jungle, so when William visits a store specialising in the supply of materials for exotic expeditions this is the first request he puts to General Cruttwell, departmental manager in what some observers have noticed bears a certain resemblance to the former Army and Navy Stores in Victoria. The Cruttwell character was a recurring one in Waugh's novels. It was the name of his tutor at Oxford, C.R.M.F. Cruttwell, who had despaired at Waugh's idle and drunken lifestyle and was rewarded with cameo appearances in several of his former student's works, invariably in an absurd and unflattering light. In this case he got off quite lightly, General Cruttwell simply dismissing William Boot's requests for cleft sticks as the work of a prankster and contenting himself with inspecting 'a newly-arrived consignment of rhinoceros-hide whips in a menacing way'.

In *Vile Bodies* the *Daily Beast* gives way to the *Daily Excess*, whose equally loathsome proprietor, Lord Monomark, congratulates Adam Symes for his gossip column which is based upon entirely fictitious events: 'Now see here Symes, I like your page. It's peppy, it's got plenty of new names in it and it's got that intimate touch.' The Daily Express Building was abandoned by its original owner when Fleet Street's newspapers emigrated to Wapping and elsewhere in the 1980s, but it remains in use, having become a London office of Goldman Sachs, an even more potent (and some would say menacing) organisation than the *Daily Beast*.

Ye Olde Cheshire Cheese, in Wine Office Court off Fleet Street, was popular with many writers including Conan Doyle, Dickens, G.K. Chesterton and John Galsworthy and the pub and its surroundings are mentioned in Galsworthy's *Forsyte Saga* and Dickens's *A Tale of Two Cities*.

No. 1 Fleet Street now belongs to the Royal Bank of Scotland whose signs on the exterior lay claim to it, but the attractive Victorian interior leaves no visitor in doubt that it remains, at heart, Child's bank with its own rich history. It has a claim to be the oldest bank in London and in *A Tale of Two Cities* it is presented as Tellson's bank, the workplace of Jarvis Lorry, who brings Dr Manette to England after his long imprisonment in the Bastille.

A Tale of Two Cities was published in 1859, the two cities being London and Paris at the time of the French Revolution. Dr Manette has been imprisoned for eighteen years in the Bastille to ensure that he remains silent about abuses committed by a French noble, the Marquis de St Evremonde. Charles Darnay, the marquis' nephew, comes to England to escape the inheritance he despises and marries Lucie, Dr Manette's daughter. Darnay returns to France and escapes execution as a former aristocrat when Sydney Carton, who has previously led a self-indulgent life, takes his place on the scaffold.

NEWGATE AND THE OLD BAILEY

Little now remains of Newgate Prison beyond the street to which it gave its name. It was demolished in 1902 to allow the expansion of its neighbour and partner in crime, the Old Bailey, Britain's most famous courthouse. It has been the scene of many of the nation's most notorious criminal trials and, of course, of the exploits of Horace Rumpole, John Mortimer's garrulous and only moderately successful criminal barrister.

Pommery's Wine Bar, which figured so prominently in the career of the late Horace Rumpole, was based on El Vino's at No. 47 Fleet Street. It was once a haunt of male journalists from the newspaper offices which abounded in the area, but protests by female journalists gained them admission, with the reluctant assent of the management in the 1970s. Since the departure of the press for Docklands and elsewhere, El Vino's is now mostly patronised by curious visitors, financiers and lawyers, many of the latter claiming to be the model for Rumpole. There used to be several El Vino wine bars, the original one dating from 1879 when Alfred Bower opened as a wine merchant in the City. The Fleet Street bar is the only survivor.

The diligent visitor can find a few remnants of the Newgate Prison in an old wall behind the Old Bailey, in a turning off Newgate Street. This wall is a relic of the fifth prison to be built on the site. The original Newgate Prison was the gatehouse of one of the entrances to the City through the Roman wall, though the gatehouse itself was built in about 1170 in the reign of Henry II and used as a prison for those awaiting trial. In the early fifteenth century this gatehouse was substantially reconstructed under the will of Richard Whittington (*c.*1359–1423), four times Lord Mayor of London, the prison being known as 'The Whit' after its benefactor.

The Dick Whittington legend itself dates from 1605 and has earned its own place in literature. It remains one of Britain's

The famous Ye Olde Cheshire Cheese pub off Fleet Street played host to many writers, such as Sir Arthur Conan Doyle, Charles Dickens and G.K. Chesterton. (Mark Beynon)

most popular pantomimes. Richard Whittington was born in the hamlet of Pauntley in Gloucestershire and was the younger son of a local knight and landowner and, as was common for younger sons at the time, was sent to London to earn his living. He became a very wealthy mercer (cloth merchant) and a member of the Mercers' Company, London's premier livery company with a magnificent hall on the corner of Iremonger Lane and Cheapside, where he is still celebrated. He paid for improvements to London's sewerage and water supply as well as for the rebuilding of Newgate. The story of Whittington and his cat is one of the few 'home-grown' pantomime tales; most others (Aladdin, Cinderella etc.) are of foreign origin. It was first staged as a pantomime in 1814, based on a play dating from the seventeenth century.

Whittington's building, which was destroyed in the Great Fire of 1666, incorporated a statue of Whittington in a niche on its exterior, the statue being accompanied by a cat. Its successor, the third Newgate, had fallen into disrepair by the 1770s and the fourth prison was in the process of being rebuilt when the almost completed building was destroyed by the Gordon rioters in 1780. Further reconstruction followed and the fifth and final Newgate, to the designs of the architect George Dance (who also designed the Mansion House), was completed in 1785. It was demolished in 1902 to allow the expansion of its neighbour the Old Bailey where, in *A Tale of Two Cities*, Charles Darnay, nephew of the notorious Marquis de St Evremonde, is acquitted of treason by reason of his resemblance to the dissolute lawyer (and later hero), Sydney Carton, who is present in court.

Newgate's notoriety as a prison and as a place from which convicted prisoners were taken to execution at Tyburn (Marble Arch) earned it a place in literature from the eighteenth century onwards, much of this being due to the compilation of the *Newgate Calendar* by the 'Keepers' (governors) of the prison. This document was originally simply a record of those entering the gaol, but keepers and others recognised that, with a little embellishment, it represented an excellent opportunity for money-making by publishing sensational accounts of the misdeeds of Newgate's inmates. It may be regarded as an early, if not the first, example of muck-raking crime reporting. Examples of the titles which were published in this way include *The Tyburn Calendar* or *Malefactors Bloody Register* (1705); *Most Notorious Highwaymen* (1719); *Plunders of the Most Noted Pirates* (1734); and, in 1780, shortly before the gaol's destruction by the Gordon rioters, *Accounts of Executions, Dying Speeches and Other Curious Particulars Relating to the Most Notorious Violaters of the Laws of their Country who have Suffered Death*. The titles may not have been catchy but the message was clear, so it is not surprising that writers of quality used the accounts as sources for their own works.

THE BEGGAR'S OPERA

The first major work to be based on Newgate was *The Beggar's Opera* by John Gay (1685–1732), which was given fresh life by the German Marxist writer Bertold Brecht as *The Threepenny Opera* during the days of the Weimar Republic in 1928. Gay's work, which appeared two centuries before Brecht's in 1728, was based on the life of Jonathan Wild (1689–1725), a notorious criminal and thief who earned money in three ways: by organising crimes carried out by others; by taking rewards from victims of crime in return for 'recovering' their stolen goods; and, most lucratively, by 'grassing' to the authorities on those who had committed crimes on his behalf. Jonathan Wild was especially hated by the populace for his role in incriminating Jack Sheppard (1702–24), who escaped four times from Newgate and thereby became a popular hero. The principal character in *The Beggar's Opera*, Peachum, is both a receiver of stolen goods and an informant, and is clearly based upon Jonathan Wild who had been executed amidst much public rejoicing three years earlier. Macheath, the highwayman ('Mack the Knife' in

Brecht's *The Threepenny Opera*) is a heroic figure who, unlike his forbear Jack Sheppard, escapes execution.

THE NEWGATE NOVEL

Such was the notoriety of Newgate in the English penal system that it spawned its own literary genre, the 'Newgate novel'. These were often based upon material found in *The Newgate Calendar*, while others drew upon personal experience of the gaol.

William Godwin (1756–1836) is remembered as the husband of Mary Wollstonecraft, author of *A Vindication of the Rights of Woman* (1790), and as the father of Mary Shelley, wife of the poet and herself author of *Frankenstein*, but Godwin himself wrote *Caleb Williams: Or Things as They Are*, an early crime novel with many references to Newgate.

Harrison Ainsworth (1805–82) wrote historical novels based on characters and episodes in the life of the prison. His novel *Rookwood* (1834) created the legend of Dick Turpin's ride to York, while *Jack Sheppard* (1839) recounts, more or less accurately, the exploits of Jack Sheppard and Jonathan Wild, each of them ending on the gallows at Tyburn. In his account of Sheppard, Ainsworth incorporates Bedlam, the asylum which holds Sheppard's insane mother. By the time that Ainsworth was writing, the Bethlehem Hospital, to give it the correct name, had been moved to Lambeth, the site now occupied by the Imperial War Museum, but Ainsworth describes it in all its horror as it would have been in Sheppard's time at Moorfields, just beyond the City boundary. Citizens were admitted to watch and listen to the unfortunate inmates, often shackled, as a form of entertainment.

Ainsworth's better-known contemporary was Edward Bulwer-Lytton (1803–73), best known for his historical novel *The Last Days of Pompeii* (1834), though in his lifetime he was better known for his Newgate novels *Paul Clifford* and *Eugene Aram*, both of them being based on events in Newgate and both breaking new ground at the time by portraying criminals not as pantomime villains but as people who engage the reader's sympathies.

William Makepeace Thackeray (1811–63) was repelled by the sympathetic light in which Lytton portrayed criminals and wrote a story called *Catherine*, which appeared in instalments in *Fraser's Magazine* in 1839–40. It was an account of a woman called Catherine Hayes, who was taken from Newgate in 1726 to be burned at Tyburn 'in very revolting circumstances' for murdering her husband. It was supposed to be a moral tale, so to strengthen the anti-criminal sentiments of the work Thackeray drew in material from other crimes of the time, including the activities of two grave-robbers who, short of corpses to be sold for dissection, drowned a young boy in Nova Scotia gardens, Bethnal Green. They then removed the dead boy's teeth with a bradawl for sale to dentists before delivering the corpse to the dissecting room of King's College Hospital where they were arrested. A sensational trial and executions followed, but Thackleray's inclusion of such notorious material in his Newgate novel did not have the desired effect and Catherine Hayes herself became an object of some sympathy.

CHARLES DICKENS AND VICTORIAN PRISONS

Thackeray, like his contemporary Charles Dickens, had formed his view of Newgate as a reporter before he wrote of it. In July 1840 both writers had, coincidentally, attended the execution of a man called Francois Courvoisier who had murdered his master, Lord Russell. The execution took place on a scaffold erected outside Newgate to which executions had been transferred from Tyburn in 1783. The transfer was made to avoid the infamous 'Tyburn Processions' in which criminals were conveyed from Newgate to Tyburn amidst much riotous and drunken behaviour. This did not, however, do much to reduce the size or conduct of the crowds who were drawn to the executions. Thackeray wrote of the experience in an account called 'On Going to See a Man Hanged', which expressed his revulsion at the experience, while Dickens was sufficiently moved by the occasion to argue that executions should take place within the prison, in private, a move that took place in 1868.

Dickens sends several of his characters to prison, drawing not only on his experience of seeing executions but on his family's own experience of the penal system. When Dickens was 12, his father John had been committed to the Marshalsea Prison in Southwark for debt, a fate to which Dickens condemned Samuel Pickwick (though in the Fleet Prison) in his first major work *The Pickwick Papers* in 1837. Twenty years later, in *Little Dorrit*, Dickens sent the whole Dorrit family to the Marshalsea following its dispute with a government department, the Circumlocution Office.

Little Dorrit was published in 1857 and draws heavily on the author's memories of the Dickens family's incarceration in the Marshalsea Prison for four months in 1824. Old William Dorrit has been imprisoned for so long in the Marshalsea that he finds it hard to imagine life outside the prison. He is comforted by the devoted care of his small daughter, Amy ('Little Dorrit') who loves, and is finally loved by, Arthur Clennam who is himself reduced to penury and joins them in the Marshalsea. William Dorrit unexpectedly inherits a large fortune which is duly lost through unwise investment with the swindling financier Merdle. William Dorrit dies and at the end of the novel Amy and Arthur, by now modestly prosperous, marry and set out on a new life together.

Dickens's criticism of the delays and obstructions of the legal system in *Little Dorrit* is second only to that shown in *Bleak House*, the 'Circumlocution Office' being the special object of his bitter satire:

> The Circumlocution Office was (as everybody knows without being told) the most important Department under Government. No public business of any kind could possibly be done at any time without the acquiescence of the Circumlocution Office. Its finger was in the largest public pie and in the smallest public tart. It was equally impossible to do the plainest right and to undo the plainest wrong without the express authority of the Circumlocution Office.

However, Dickens's most memorable prison scenes were set in Newgate itself, which he had visited many times as a journalist before witnessing Courvoisier's execution. Newgate makes many appearances in *Oliver Twist*. Oliver is led past Newgate by Sikes and Nancy, with the experience made more sinister by the heavy mist and rain in which Dickens sets the episode. In the light of a gas lamp from a shop window Oliver notices Nancy's pale face, lined with fear of Sikes. One of Dickens's darkest passages of the book describes Fagin in his death cell at Newgate. In this early work the contrasts are particularly marked between the virtuous and incorruptible Oliver and his evil tormentors, Fagin and Sikes. Fagin's trial at the Old Bailey, next to Newgate, is attended by spectators whose 'looks expressive of abhorrence' are directed towards Fagin in the dock, and when the judge pronounces the death sentence for his numerous crimes Fagin hears 'a peal of joy from the populace outside, greeting the news that he would die on Monday'. Oliver visits Fagin in the condemned cell and sees his face 'retaining no human expression but rage and terror' and showing indignation at his plight rather than regret for his misdeeds. The cell door and other Newgate relics may now be seen in the Museum of London. As he leaves Newgate, Oliver sees the world outside where 'everything told of life and animation but one dark cluster of objects in the centre of all – the black stage, the cross beam, the rope and all the hideous apparatus of death'. The bells of St Sepulchre, whose tolling signalled to the condemned the approach of the hour of execution, are heard by Oliver as he leaves Newgate.

St Sepulchre, the City of London's largest parish church, is celebrated in the rhyme 'Oranges and Lemons' as the Bells of Old Bailey ('When will you pay me? Say the Bells of Old Bailey') and its 'execution bell' is on view in a glass case in the south aisle of the church. Bill Sikes is saved from execution only because, while fleeing after killing Nancy, he falls and is hanged at Jacob's Island, a notorious rookery in Bermondsey on the present site of Jacob Street, SE1, situated on the appropriately named Dickens Estate. When Winston Smith in 1984 recalls the rhyme, he can 'hear the bells of a lost London that still existed somewhere or other, disguised and forgotten'.

Dickens also writes of the Old Bailey in *Great Expectations*, where Pip's benefactor Magwitch, having returned from deportation to Australia, is caught and, for that crime, condemned to death. Magwitch stands in the dock at the Old Bailey, Pip leaning over the rail to hold his hand, as Magwitch, with other convicts, watches the judge don the black cap and pronounce sentence. Pip tells the reader:

> Penned in the dock, as I stood outside it at the corner with his hand in mine, were the two-and-thirty men and women: some defiant, some stricken with terror, some sobbing and weeping, some covering their faces, some staring gloomily about. There had been shrieks from among the women convicts but they had been stilled and a hush had succeeded.

Magwitch tells the judge: 'My Lord, I have received my sentence of death from the Almighty but I bow to yours,' though he escapes execution when he dies of injuries sustained in a murderous final struggle with his nemesis and former partner in crime.

ANOTHER NEWGATE NOVEL

The most famous Newgate novel is probably that of Daniel Defoe (1660–1731), better known as the author of *Robinson Crusoe*, who spent a short time in Newgate because of a satirical pamphlet he wrote about the established Church. His Newgate novel bore the full title *The Fortunes and Misfortunes of the Famous Moll Flanders who was Born in Newgate and During a Life of Continued Variety for Threescore Years was Twelve Years a Whore, Five Times a Wife (whereof once to her own Brother), Twelve Years a Thief, Eight Years a Transported Felon in Virginia, at Last Grew Rich, Lived Honest and Died a Penitent*. Having read the title one hardly needs to read the book. In the novel, better known simply as *Moll Flanders*, Defoe makes use of his (and Moll's) intimate knowledge of London's streets to show how Moll plied her trade as seducer and thief to avoid detection. Thus, having stolen 'a gold watch, a silk purse of gold, his sword and fine snuff box' from a client, she leaps from the carriage in which they are travelling and escapes into 'the narrow streets beyond Temple Bar'.

TEMPLE BAR AND ST PAUL'S

At that time Temple Bar stood in the Strand, which marked the boundary between the City of London and Westminster. It was surrounded by dark alleys into which Moll could escape and was known to Defoe because he had spent time in the pillory there for his satirical pamphlet, though a supportive crowd meant he was only pelted with flowers. Temple Bar was dismantled in 1878 to improve the Strand as a thoroughfare and in 2004 it was re-erected as the entrance to Paternoster Square, adjacent to the north-west end of St Paul's Cathedral.

Since Tudor times Paternoster Row, at the top of Ludgate Hill, has been associated with the sale of stationery and books. After the Great Fire of 1666 other traders like mercers moved out and it became almost exclusively devoted to bookselling and publishing, *Robinson Crusoe* being published from there in 1719. The area was devastated by bombing in the Second World War, when 6 million books were destroyed. It was rebuilt and reopened as Paternoster Square, the Temple Bar being retrieved from an ignoble site near Cheshunt in Hertfordshire and re-erected as an entrance to the square in 2004.

The present St Paul's, the work of Christopher Wren, is the fifth cathedral on the site and was completed in 1710 following the destruction of the medieval cathedral in the Great Fire of 1666. By the time of the fire, the earlier building was in a poor state. It had long been in need of refurbishment and its condition had not been improved by its use for quartering Parliamentary troops during the civil war of the 1640s. In his poem '*Annus Mirabilis*: the Year of Wonders 1666' Dryden referred to the destruction of the cathedral as a providential act following its use for such a purpose:

> The daring flames peeped in and saw from far
> The awful beauties of the sacred quire:
> But since it was prophaned by Civil War
> Heaven thought it fit to have it purged by fire.

Charlotte Brontë is most often associated with Haworth, Yorkshire, but she visited her publisher in London and presumably also visited St Paul's Cathedral since she sends her heroine Villette there:

> Finding myself before St Paul's, I went in; I mounted the dome whence I saw London, with its river, and its bridges, and its churches; I saw antique Westminster and the green Temple Gardens, with sun upon them, and a glad blue sky of early spring above.

COLDBATH FIELDS

Newgate was not the only London prison which was celebrated in literature. Another was Coldbath Fields, London's largest prison, which accommodated 1,200 inmates. It had existed since the sixteenth century and was extensively rebuilt and enlarged in the nineteenth century as part of the Victorian prison reform programme. Unlike Newgate it adopted the 'silent and solitary' regime whereby prisoners were denied all contact with other inmates in the belief that this would prevent one prisoner from 'infecting' another with his own bad habits and also that a solitary existence would oblige prisoners to reflect upon their errors and mend their ways. Many became deranged as a result of the experience and such was the reputation of the prison that Coleridge wrote in his poem 'The Devil's Thoughts', describing the devil's feelings as he passed the prison:

> As he went through Coldbath Fields he saw
> A solitary cell,
> And the Devil was pleased, for it gave him a hint
> For improving his prisons in Hell.

The prison was demolished in 1889 to make way for the Royal Mail's Mount Pleasant sorting office and is remembered by the adjacent Cold Bath Square, EC1.

Dickens treats some other prisoners better than he treats Fagin. In *The Old Curiosity Shop* the innocent errand boy Kit Nubbles, who is devoted to Little Nell, is framed by the evil dwarf Quilp and briefly imprisoned, but Dickens reassures his readers that Kit is 'lodged like some few others in the gaol, apart from the masses of prisoners because he was not supposed to be utterly depraved and irreclaimable'. Even Uriah Heep in *David Copperfield* becomes a model prisoner following his unmasking by Wilkins Micawber. However, the work in which Newgate figures most prominently is undoubtedly *Barnaby Rudge*.

Barnaby Rudge, or, to give its full title, *Barnaby Rudge: A Tale of the Riots of 'Eighty* was published in 1841 and of all Dickens's works it is the one most firmly based on historical events. The Gordon Riots were led by a renegade and highly disturbed aristocrat called Lord George Gordon, third son of the Duke of Gordon, in protest at the Catholic Relief Act of 1778 which enabled Roman Catholics to join the army and own and inherit property. These reasonable enough measures outraged Gordon, whose speeches in Parliament prompted one fellow Parliamentarian to comment that 'the noble lord has got a twist in his head, a certain whirligig which runs away with him if anything relative to religion is mentioned'. In June 1780 a crowd of Gordon's supporters, numbering in excess of 20,000, assembled in Lambeth and proceeded to Westminster carrying banners bearing the message 'No Popery'. The headquarters of the rioters was the Boot Tavern in Cromer Street, Bloomsbury, which still exists – though the original building has been replaced by the present one. The mob briefly invaded the Palace of Westminster before being repulsed, and proceeded to attack Catholic chapels of foreign embassies, followed by the home of the Lord Chief Justice, Lord Mansfield, at 29 Bloomsbury Square. The riots continued for four days and culminated in an attack on Newgate, where some of their number had earlier been incarcerated. Dickens's story follows the disturbances quite closely with the fictional and villainous Sir John Chester helping to foment the riots; the simpleton Barnaby Rudge being innocently drawn into them and narrowly escaping execution; and the fate of Ned Dennis, the treacherous Tyburn hangman, reflecting Dickens's own ambivalent feelings about capital punishment.

The attack on Newgate was witnessed by the poet George Crabbe, who paid a householder sixpence to watch the spectacle from his roof, commenting: 'Here I saw a new species of gaol delivery. The captives marched out with all the honours of war, accompanied by a musical band of rattling fetters.' William Blake also watched the rioters from his new printing shop in Broad Street. The mob was eventually dispelled by troops and twenty-one rioters were hanged, Lord George Gordon escaping a charge of treason on the grounds that his intentions were peaceful and he couldn't be held responsible for the excesses of misguided supporters. After a spell in the Tower of London, Gordon ended his days in Newgate having been convicted of libelling the Queen of France, Marie Antoinette. In Newgate he converted to the Jewish faith.

Dickens was born in 1812, thirty-two years after the riots, but he must have had contact with people who remembered them, so vivid and authentic is his account. The principal character of Dickens's tale, Barnaby Rudge, is drawn into the riots by being encouraged to carry one of their colourful flags and he is sent to Newgate where, fettered in his dark cell, he was depicted by Dickens's illustrator Phiz in one of his most famous illustrations.

Phiz, whose real name was Hablot Knight Browne (1815–82), was of French Huguenot descent and became Dickens's illustrator in 1836 when the notoriously irascible writer fell out with Robert Seymour, who had illustrated *The Pickwick Papers*. Browne illustrated ten of Dickens's novels and his easy temperament enabled him to accommodate the novelist's uneven temper, the collaboration lasting almost a quarter of a century to 1860. He also illustrated works by other Newgate novelists, including Harrison Ainsworth and Edward Bulwer-Lytton. He is commemorated by a Blue Plaque at his former home, 239 Ladbroke Grove.

Barnaby was released from Newgate by the rioters, recaptured and condemned to death, but reprieved at the eleventh hour. Hugh the Ostler, another character in the novel, is hanged as his gypsy mother had been before him and his behaviour as he approaches the scaffold outside Newgate is defiant as he cries:

> Upon these human shambles I, who never raised a hand in prayer till now, call down the wrath of God! On that black tree of which I am the ripened fruit I do invoke the curse of all its victims past, and present and to come.

As eight o'clock approaches, the hour of execution, the crowd swells 'with every chime of St Sepulchre's clock' and as the condemned are brought from the gaol the cry of 'Hats off' is heard, as Dickens himself had heard it at Courvoisier's execution in 1840, the year before *Barnaby Rudge* was written. Dickens shows sympathy for all the executed except the hangman Dennis, who is portrayed as a coward cravenly begging for a reprieve. Dickens concludes that 'those who suffered as rioters were for the most part the weakest, meanest and most miserable amongst them' and adds a moving account of a weeping, grey-haired man approaching the scaffold and embracing his son as the boy goes to his death.

SMITHFIELD

Smithfield is frequently mentioned in the works of Dickens. It takes its name from the 'Smooth Field', which was located just outside the City wall. In Sir Thomas More's *Utopia*, an account of an imaginary ideal society, the killing of animals takes place outside the City walls, reflecting practices at Smithfield. From the twelfth century, sales of live animals took place here alongside Bartholomew Fair, which was mostly concerned with the sale of cloth and occurred during August each year following St Bartholomew's Day, the patron of the nearby hospital of that name. It is remembered in the name of the neighbouring street, Cloth Fair. Ben Jonson's play *Bartholomew Fair*, written in 1614, described some of the fair's attractions: 'The wonder of nature, a girl about sixteen years of age, born in Cheshire and not above eighteen inches long' and 'a Man with one head and two distinct bodies.'

Wordsworth also described Bartholomew Fair in Book VII of his autobiographical poem *The Prelude* entitled 'Residence in London':

> The silver-collared Negro with his timbrel,
> Equestrians, tumblers, women, girls, and boys,
> Blue-breeched, pink-vested, and with towering plumes.—
> All moveables of wonder, from all parts,
> Are here—Albinos, painted Indians, Dwarfs,
> The Horse of knowledge, and the learned Pig,
> The Stone-eater, the Man that swallows fire,
> Giants, Ventriloquists, the Invisible Girl,
> The Bust that speaks, and moves its goggling eyes,
> The Wax-work, Clock-work, all the marvellous craft
> Of modern Merlins, Wild Beasts, Puppet-shows,
> All out-o'-the-way, far-fetched, perverted things,
> All freaks of nature, all Promethean thoughts
> Of man; his dulness, madness, and their feats
> All jumbled up together to make up
> This Parliament of Monsters.

By the mid-nineteenth century the fair and the cattle market had become notorious for disorderly behaviour, the phrase 'bull in a china shop' deriving from the practice of goading animals to fury by the huge crowds that gathered there during the fair. In 1855 the fair was suppressed for that reason and the market became one for slaughtered meat only, as it is today.

Dickens would have been familiar with its reputation for misbehaviour and it is perhaps for this reason that he often uses it as a setting for disorder. In *Oliver Twist*, Oliver is led by Nancy and Sikes through Smithfield, which is full of 'crowding, pushing, driving, beating, unwashed, unshaven dirty figures', while Pip, in *Great Expectations*, declares that 'the shameful place, being all asmear with filth and fat and blood and foam, seemed to stick to me'. But it is also in *Great Expectations* that Pip sees the lawyer Jaggers, who informs Pip of his 'Great Expectations' at his office in Little Britain behind St Bartholomew's Hospital.

Just to the south of Smithfield is Snow Hill, the London headquarters of Wackford Squeers, the brutal and sadistic headmaster of Dotheboys Hall in *Nicholas Nickleby*. It is now the site of a police station of the City of London Police, Snow Hill being one of three police stations of this, Britain's smallest police service.

CLOTH FAIR

Just to the south of Little Britain, 43 Cloth Fair was for many years the home of the poet John Betjeman who celebrated London in many of his poems. Despite his residence within the City he was often critical of those who earned their living there. In his poem 'The City' he wrote of:

> Businessmen with awkward hips
> And dirty jokes upon their lips
> And large behinds and jingling chains
> And riddled teeth and riddling brains...

And:

> Young men who wear on office stools
> The ties of minor public schools...

It is hardly an affectionate portrait!

A sadder note is struck on his 'Monody' on the death of Aldersgate Street station, which was written when the old station, close to his home in Cloth Fair, was redeveloped and incorporated into the new Barbican scheme, whose multi-storey dwellings replaced the devastation caused by bombing in the Second World War. A 'Monody' is simply a poem of lamentation written to mark a death and here John Betjeman applies it to the old station, now known as 'Barbican':

> Snow falls in the buffet of Aldersgate station,
> Soot hangs in the tunnel in clouds of steam.
> City of London! before the next desecration
> Let your steepled forest of churches be my theme.

This, the first verse, looks back to the time when the Metropolitan Railway, a Victorian invention, was powered by steam trains and thus celebrates three of the poet's greatest loves: the Victorians, steam railways and the Metropolitan Railway which, in 'Summoned by Bells', he celebrated at length in verse:

> Great was our joy, Ronald Hughes Wright's and mine
> To travel by the Underground all day
> Between the rush hours, so that very soon
> There was no station, north to Finsbury Park,
> To Barking eastwards, Clapham Common south,
> No temporary platform in the west
> Among the Actons and the Ealings where
> We had not once alighted. Metroland
> Beckoned us out to lanes in Beechy Bucks.

4

THE INNS OF COURT

Inns of Court enjoy the exclusive privilege to admit students as barristers, with the accompanying right to appear as advocates in the senior courts of England and Wales. Lincoln's Inn, the oldest, is recorded from 1422, Middle Temple from 1501, Inner Temple from 1505 and Gray's Inn from 1569, though it is likely that they all date from the fourteenth century. They are called 'Inns' because they originally provided accommodation for students, but their function is now educational, preparing students for work at the bar (hence the term 'barristers') through lectures and strange rituals which require students to eat a certain number of dinners in the magnificent and historic halls of the Inns. They frequently feature in novels, especially during the Victorian period, not least because writers like Dickens often learned their trade as court reporters and worked in one or other of the Inns. A separate category embraced the Inns of Chancery, which were numerous but began to disappear during the nineteenth century as the Law Society took over the training of solicitors.

LINCOLN'S INN

Just to the south of High Holborn we find Lincoln's Inn Fields where, in *The Warden*, Trollope places the chambers of the Attorney-General, Sir Abraham Haphazard. At Lincoln's Inn the great man is visited by the Reverend Septimus Harding, the principal character of *The Warden*, who has decided that he should give up the wardenship of Hiram's Hospital, which he enjoys and which provides him with a comfortable living, although the law would support his right to retain the office. With great difficulty he persuades the lawyer that his conscience is more important to him than any legal niceties while knowing that, although his daughter Eleanor will support his decision, he must now explain it to his very unsympathetic son-in-law Archdeacon Grantly:

> Mr Harding was sufficiently satisfied with the interview to feel a glow of comfort as he descended into the small old square of Lincoln's Inn. It was a calm, bright, beautiful night, and by the light of the moon, even the chapel of Lincoln's Inn, and the sombre row of chambers, which surround the quadrangle, looked well. He stood still a moment to collect his thoughts, and reflect on what he had done, and was about to do. He knew that the attorney-general regarded him as little better than a fool, but that he did not mind; he and the attorney-general had not much in common between them; he knew also that others, whom he did care about, would think so too; but Eleanor, he was sure, would exult in what he had done, and the bishop, he trusted, would sympathise with him.
>
> In the meantime he had to meet the archdeacon, and so he walked slowly down Chancery Lane and along Fleet Street, feeling sure that his work for the night was not yet over. When he reached the hotel he rang the bell

> quietly, and with a palpitating heart; he almost longed to escape round the corner, and delay the coming storm by a further walk round St Paul's Churchyard, but he heard the slow creaking shoes of the old waiter approaching, and he stood his ground manfully.

There are many Dickens associations in the area, much of the action in *Bleak House* being set in Lincoln's Inn. The premises of the sinister and blackmailing lawyer Tulkinghorn are at 58 Lincoln's Inn Fields, described as 'a large house, formerly a house of state let off in sets of chambers now and in those shrunken fragments of greatness lawyers lie like maggots in nuts'. It was in reality well known to Dickens as the home of his friend and biographer John Forster. In the same novel, Guppy, the admirer of Esther Summerson, works in an office at Lincoln's Inn Fields in the practice of the long-winded 'Conversation' Kenge and his partner Carboy. Moreover, the Court of Chancery, in which the endless case of Jarndyce and Jarndyce is hopelessly mired, is based at Lincoln's Inn in Dickens's *Bleak House*. Across Chancery Lane from Lincoln's Inn, off Cursitor Street, is Took's Court, represented in the same novel as Cook's Court where Mr Snagsby has his Law Stationery shop.

GRAY'S INN

Dickens worked for a while in a firm of attorneys in Gray's Inn to the north, in 'a poor old set of chambers in three rooms' in South Square, where he later placed Tommy Traddles's chambers in *David Copperfield*. His office later moved to 6 Raymond Buildings. In his essay 'The Uncommercial Traveller' he described Gray's Inn in harsh terms:

> I look upon Gray's Inn generally as one of the most depressing institutions in bricks and mortar known to

> the children of men. Can anything be more dreary than its arid Square, Sahara Desert of the law, with the ugly old tiled-topped tenements, the dirty windows, the bills To Let, the door-posts inscribed like gravestones, the crazy gateway giving upon the filthy Lane, the scowling iron-barred prison-like passage into Verulam buildings.

Some of these features may still be seen, though most visitors find Gray's Inn a tranquil and attractive quarter of London. To the east, south of Holborn Circus, is Thavies Inn, no longer an Inn of Chancery, where the chaotic Jellyby family lived and where they provided a night's rest for Esther, Ada and Richard in *Bleak House*. Dickens himself lived for a time in rooms at Furnival's Inn, another Inn of Chancery, which was on the present site of Holborn Bars (still often referred to as the 'Prudential Building') and was joined there by his wife Catherine shortly after their marriage.

Samuel Pickwick's legal adviser, Perker, has chambers at Gray's Inn from where he conducts the defence which results in Pickwick losing his breach of promise case in Bardell vs Pickwick. David Copperfield also stays in Gray's Inn for a while.

Gray's Inn itself has an important place in literature since Shakespeare's early play *A Comedy of Errors* was first performed in its Hall at Christmas.

A little further to the south is Portugal Street, in which is to be found 'The George', public house, successor to 'The Magpie and Stump' which was one of the haunts of Samuel Pickwick in *The Pickwick Papers*.

Another resident of Portugal Street was John Wilmot, Earl of Rochester (1647–80), a poet noted for his scurrilous and salacious verses and who was the subject of 'Lord Rochester's Monkey' by Graham Greene (1904–91).

Nearby is 'The Old Curiosity Shop', home of Little Nell in Dickens's novel of that name. The shop is in Portsmouth Street, close to Clare Market, which was well known to Dickens since

The Old Curiosity Shop, immortalised by the Charles Dickens novel. (Mark Beynon)

he had dealings with a bookbinder there. It was also the home of Johnson's Alamode Beef House, where Dickens lunched during his blacking warehouse days and where David Copperfield later did the same. The model for Dickens's shop was some distance away in Orange Street, behind the National Gallery, but the nineteenth-century owner of the shop in Portsmouth Street, a former dairy dating from the sixteenth century, changed the name of his antiques and bric-a-brac shop to 'The Old Curiosity Shop' to take advantage of the popularity of Dickens's novel and the author's association with the area. Dickens asserted in his novel that 'the old house had long ago been pulled down', but the house in Portsmouth Street continues to attract curious visitors.

The Old Curiosity Shop, published in 1841, tells the story of Little Nell Trent, who devotedly cares for her grandfather who barely scrapes a living from his Old Curiosity Shop, a task made harder by spendthrift relatives and by the machinations of one of Dickens's most sinister characters, the moneylending dwarf Daniel Quilp, who eventually seizes the shop. Grandfather and Nell flee and find refuge in a country cottage, where they are discovered by the grandfather's brother, too late for Little Nell who has died. Kit Nubbles, Little Nell's devoted admirer employed at the Old Curiosity Shop, attracts the hostility of the evil Quilp, who tries to frame him as a thief, but his deceit comes to light and Quilp dies whilst fleeing his pursuers. Like many of Dickens's novels, *The Old Curiosity Shop* was published in weekly episodes (in Dickens's magazine *Master Humphrey's Clock*) and it is recorded that crowds gathered by the quayside in New York to obtain the latest instalments as they arrived from England. The passage describing the death of Little Nell attracted unprecedented attention, though it was later criticised for excess of pathos. Oscar Wilde declared that: 'One would have to have a heart of stone to read the death of Little Nell without dissolving into tears … of laughter.'

THE MIDDLE AND INNER TEMPLE

The Temple, which lies between Fleet Street and the river, is an area rich in history, including that of literature. It lies on the western border of the City of London where it meets the City of Westminster. It was here that, according to Shakespeare, in *Henry VI Part I*, the two factions contending the Wars of the Roses gathered and declared their allegiance to one side or the other by plucking a white rose, to represent the house of York, or a red rose to represent the claims of Lancaster. The two factions are represented by Richard Plantagenet, later Duke of York, and John Beaufort, later Duke of Somerset:

Plantagenet: Let him that is a true-born gentleman
And stands upon the honour of his birth,
If he suppose that I have pleaded truth
From off this brier pluck a white rose
with me.
Beaufort: Let him that is no coward nor no flatterer,
But dare maintain the party of the truth,
Pluck a red rose from off this thorn with me.

There is no evidence that this event ever occurred, in the garden of the Temple church or elsewhere, but it was taken up by Sir Walter Scott in his now forgotten historical novel *Anne of Geierstein*, or *The Maiden of the Mist* (1829), in which the expression 'Wars of the Roses' was first used and from there it made its way into history books and legends.

In Dickens's *Great Expectations*, Pip and his friend Herbert Pocket take chambers in the Temple, in Garden Court, where he is visited by Magwitch who tells him of his fortune. Pip's final meeting with Magwitch occurs there on a stormy night when 'a vast heavy veil had been driving over London from the East, and it drove still, as if in the East there were an Eternity of cloud and wind', weather which presages

Magwitch's fate. At Temple Stairs Pip also keeps the boat with which he later hopes to effect Magwitch's escape.

Nearby Fountain Court remains an attractive feature of this part of London and appears in better weather and happier circumstances in *The Adventures of Martin Chuzzlewit* as a place where Ruth Pinch and John Westlock meet:

> Brilliantly the Temple Fountain sparkled in the sun and laughingly its liquid music played, and merrily the idle drops of water danced and danced, and peeping out in sport among the trees, plunged lightly down to hide themselves, as little Ruth and her companion came towards it.

John Galsworthy had chambers at 3 Paper Buildings, Inner Temple in the 1890s and, although he barely practised as a barrister, his legal training is reflected in *The Forsyte Saga*, much of which is concerned with legal actions. Paper Buildings also held the chambers of Sir John Chester in *Barnaby Rudge* and Mr Stryver in *A Tale of Two Cities*.

Temple Underground station also claims to be the place where Baroness Orczy, while queuing for a ticket, conceived the idea of *The Scarlet Pimpernel*, her best-known work, though it should be added that Tower Hill station has a rival claim to that honour.

The Temple is also the London residence of Tom Towers, editor of *The Jupiter* (a thinly disguised caricature of *The Times*) who, in Trollope's *The Warden*, supports the campaign to reform the charity Hiram's Hospital, of which the Revd Septimus Harding is the warden of the title. The cause is taken up by other journalists, notably the self-righteous Dr Pessimist Anticant, and Mr Popular Sentiment, caricatures of Thomas Carlyle and Charles Dickens respectively. It is in the Temple that Septimus Harding visits Tom Towers, who is disconcerted by the quiet clergyman's wild hand gestures, a habit he had formed when nervous of playing his much-loved, but on this occasion imaginary, cello.

5

THE CITY OF WESTMINSTER

COVENT GARDEN

Covent Garden, formerly the site of London's principal fruit and vegetable market, has many literary associations, both fictional and real. Eliza Doolittle, the heroine of Bernard Shaw's play *Pygmalion* and of its musical adaptation *My Fair Lady*, was a Covent Garden flower seller, while Bow Street, Covent Garden, was the home of the magistrates' court from which the novelist Henry Fielding (1707–54) and his brother John dispensed justice untainted by bribery. This was a new phenomenon in eighteenth-century London, employing Britain's first effective police force, the Bow Street Runners. Two of the Runners appear in *Oliver Twist* and *Great Expectations* as Blathers and Duff. In *Oliver Twist*, Dickens sends the pickpocket the Artful Dodger before the magistrates in Bow Street for one of his many court appearances. The most famous magistrates' court in the world closed its doors for the last time on 14 July 2006, its work being transferred to Westminster Magistrates' Court in Horseferry Road. The adjoining Bow Street police station, with its unique white lamp, closed at the same time. (Queen Victoria had commanded a white lamp be used instead of a blue one, as the blue reminded her of the room in which Albert died.)

The Theatre Royal, Covent Garden, first opened in 1732, the proprietor being John Rich, who paid for it from the proceeds of *The Beggar's Opera* (see reference on page 49). It was the most luxurious theatre ever built in London and saw the first production of many of Handel's works and of *She Stoops to Conquer* by Oliver Goldsmith in 1773. The author was so worried about the reception of his work that for the first night he persuaded many of his friends to attend and applaud, and he could not himself bear to watch the production until the final act. It was a great success and made Goldsmith's name. In 1775 *The Rivals* by Richard Sheridan was first produced there. In 1808 the theatre burned down and when it reopened the following year prices were put up to pay for the rebuilding, setting off the Old Price Riots, which continued for sixty-one nights before the management gave way. It staged the first performances in English of Mozart's *Don Giovanni* (1817) and *The Marriage of Figaro* (1819) before being burned down again in 1856. The third theatre reopened in 1858 and was extended and refurbished in the 1980s. It is now devoted to the production of opera and ballet, and has witnessed the premieres of many twentieth century works by composers like Benjamin Britten, Sir Arthur Bliss, Ralph Vaughan Williams and William Walton.

Bow Street Magistrates' Court also appears in Anthony Trollope's Palliser series of novels when, in *Phineas Redux*, Phineas Finn, who is making his way up the Parliamentary ladder, survives the attempt by a jealous husband to shoot him, but is then accused of murdering the President of the Board of Trade, the unpleasant Mr Bonteen. Having been questioned at Bow Street he is sent to Newgate Prison prior to trial at the Old Bailey, but is saved when his admirer, the wealthy widow Madame Max Goesler, unmasks the true culprit, the wily preacher the Revd Joseph Emilius. Phineas later marries Madame Max.

To the west of Bow Street, linking it to Covent Garden Market, is Russell Street, which was formerly the site of the burial ground of St Mary le Strand, the church itself being located in the Strand, opposite Somerset House. This constricted site was probably in the mind of Charles Dickens when he described a 'hemmed-in churchyard, pestiferous and obscene' in *Bleak House* as the burial place of the wretched Captain Hawdon and the run-down area as the home of Tom-all-Alone.

On the opposite side of Covent Garden, leading west from the market itself, is Henrietta Street, long the home of publishers, including the firm of Chapman and Hall after their move from the Strand. Besides the works of Dickens they also published those of Evelyn Waugh, whose father, Arthur Waugh was for many years the firm's managing director.

In *Vile Bodies*, first published by Chapman and Hall in 1930, reference is made to a publisher (unnamed) in Henrietta Street with a young director called Benfleet, who attributes all his harshest decisions to his fellow-director 'Old Rampole', supposedly a ruthless and tyrannical martinet. Benfleet, alone in his office, reflects how fortunate it is that his authors never meet Old Rampole, 'that benign old gentleman who once a week drove up to board meetings from the country, whose chief interest in the business was confined to the progress of a little book of his own about bee-keeping'. It is hard to avoid the conclusion that this is an uncharacteristically kind reference to Waugh's endlessly patient father who had financed Waugh's dissolute progress through Oxford, was noted for his calm and benevolent nature (so different from that of his son) and by 1930 was semi-retired from the business.

To the north of Henrietta Street, forming a link between Floral Street and Garrick Street, is the short stretch of Rose Street, which contains one of London's most historic pubs, the Lamb and Flag. The present building dates from 1623, though an earlier tavern probably existed on the site, making it possibly

London's oldest pub. At one time the pub was known locally as the Bucket of Blood because of the bare-knuckle fights which took place in this rather disreputable area of London, and in 1679 the poet John Dryden was beaten up by thugs hired by John Wilmot, Earl of Rochester, whom the poet had offended. A Dryden bar, named in the poet's honour, is on the first floor and the pub was also popular with Charles Dickens.

Further to the west, still on the Covent Garden side of Charing Cross Road, is the Ambassadors theatre, which occupies a small place in our literary history, since for twenty-three years, 1952–75, it was the home of the play *The Mousetrap* by Agatha Christie. It transferred to the nearby St Martin's theatre where it continues to attract audiences well into its second half century. Further down St Martin's Lane is the Duke of York's theatre, which staged the first productions of J.M. Barrie's plays *The Admirable Crichton* (1902) and *Peter Pan* (1904), the latter running every Christmas until 1914.

MARYLEBONE

Baker Street, of course, is principally remembered as the home of the world's most famous detective, at No. 221B, where Sherlock Holmes, over several pipes, would ponder the mysteries that were laid before him in the *Strand Magazine*. There also, cared for by the landlady Mrs Hudson, the faithful Dr Watson informed readers of *The Musgrave Ritual* that Holmes kept 'his cigars in the coal scuttle, his tobacco in the toe end of a Persian slipper, and his unanswered correspondence transfixed by a jack knife into the very centre of his wooden mantelpiece'. Since the appearance of the first Holmes story in 1887, in *A Study in Scarlet*, readers have been addressing letters to 221B, undeterred by the fact that when the stories were first written the numbers did not run beyond 100 and that 221B has never existed as a postal address. Some have identified No. 61 as the

The fictional 221B Baker Street is now home to the famous Sherlock Holmes Museum. (Mark Beynon)

model for the detective's lodgings, an address that did exist when the stories were written. The Abbey National Building Society long occupied the site where the address would have been and shouldered the burden of answering the detective's correspondence. In 1990 the Sherlock Holmes Museum, at 239 Baker Street, unveiled a plaque stating that it was 'officially' No. 221B. It is open every day except Christmas Day. Nearby is a shop advertising Hudson's Soap, the implication being that it was used by Holmes's famous landlady. A similar claim is made by the Sherlock Holmes pub in Northumberland Avenue, off Trafalgar Square. The pub changed its name after the 1951 Festival of Britain when Sherlock Holmes's flat, installed on the South Bank site of the festival as a visitor attraction, was dismantled and installed in the former Northumberland Arms where, in *The Hound of the Baskervilles*, two of Sir Henry Baskerville's boots mysteriously disappeared.

Conan Doyle became dismayed at the fact that his fictional detective, whom he considered to be a minor creation, became so popular that he put the author's other works in the shade. Accordingly he decided to kill him off and duly did so when Sherlock Holmes apparently fell to his death in the *Reichenbach Falls*, Switzerland, carrying with him the criminal mastermind Professor Moriarty in *The Adventure of the Final Problem*, published in 1893. A plaque close to the falls records the event. Readers, however, were outraged and demanded the return of Holmes, who was duly revived and featured in Conan Doyle's most famous story, *The Hound of the Baskervilles*, published in instalments in the *Strand Magazine* from August 1901.

Baker Street has a further claim to literary fame since it was to lodgings in Baker Street that the unctuous and hypocritical clergyman Obadiah Slope retired after he failed in his machinations to become Dean of Barchester in Trollope's *Barchester Towers*. Mrs Proudie, the wife of the Bishop of Barchester, triumphed, but Slope survived to marry a wealthy widow and become Archdeacon of London with a parish church near the top of Baker Street.

East of Baker Street, on the south side of Marylebone Road, is the parish church of Marylebone, St Mary's, built in the classical style by Thomas Hardwick. At the time that he was conceiving *Dombey and Son*, Charles Dickens was living nearby at 1 Devonshire Terrace, and it appears that it was this church which Dickens had in mind, with its characteristic 'steeple clock', as the church where many of the novel's more dismal events unfold.

Dombey and Son was published in 1848 and is one of the saddest of Dickens's works. The story opens with the birth of Paul Dombey, only son of the head of the shipping house of Dombey and Son, his mother dying following childbirth. Dombey senior is a rich, proud and insensitive man who invests all his hopes and feelings in his new son and neglects his affectionate daughter Florence. The boy, always delicate, sickens and dies, which drives the father further from feelings for his daughter. He exiles to the West Indies a young employee, Walter Gay, who loves Florence and Dombey's second marriage is a disaster when his young wife leaves him. The Dombey business fails and Gay returns from the West Indies and marries Florence, who is reconciled to her father in his desolation. One of the colourful minor characters is Captain Cuttle, 'a gentleman in a wide suit of blue, with a hook instead of a hand attached to his right wrist'.

The events set at the church include the funeral of Paul Dombey's wife and mother of his son, also Paul; young Paul's gloomy baptism, briefly delayed by a short interval to allow a marriage of an ill-matched bride and groom; the funeral of young Paul; and the scene of Mr Dombey's second, disastrous marriage. Bryanston Square, a short walk from the church, has been identified as the home of the Dombeys 'on the shady side of a tall, dark, dreadfully genteel street … a house of dismal state with a circular back to it.'

A short distance to the west of the church is Baker Street station, the former headquarters of the Metropolitan Railway, surmounted by Chiltern Court, the highly fashionable residences erected above the station which opened in 1932 and whose tenants included Arnold Bennett and H.G. Wells. For the buffet at Baker Street John Betjeman composed a poem detailing a husband and wife meeting there, he after a day's work, she after a day's shopping:

> Early electric! Sit you down and see,
> 'Mid this fine woodwork and a smell of dinner,
> A stained-glass windmill and a pot of tea,
> And sepia views of leafy lanes in PINNER …

Though he ends on a sad note:

> Cancer has killed him. Heart is killing her …
> Of all their loves and hopes on hurrying feet
> Thou art the worn memorial, Baker Street.

A DANDY AND A DOCTOR

To the east, at the top of Regent Street, the Langham Hotel lies in Portland Place, opposite the present home of the BBC at Broadcasting House. It was the scene of one of literature's most productive meetings. It was built between 1863 and 1865 at the colossal cost of £300,000 and featured such luxuries as a hundred water closets and thirty-six bathrooms for its 380 rooms. Its original owners over-stretched themselves and had to sell it for little more than half the cost of its construction, but under new management it became profitable and began to attract such guests as Mark Twain, the Czech composer Antonin Dvorak and the Italian conductor Toscanini, who conducted concerts at the nearby Queen's Hall, home of the early Promenade Concerts. But its claim to literary fame lies in a meeting arranged on 30 August 1889 by the American literary agent Joseph Marshall Stoddart, who had heard of two up-and-coming authors and wanted to commission works from them for his publication *Lippincott's Monthly Magazine*. The first was beginning to establish himself as a playwright, story-teller and raconteur and evidently arrived for the meeting like a 'languorous dandy'. His name was Oscar Wilde. The second would-be author was a doctor whose attempts to develop his medical practice at 2 Devonshire Place were described by himself: 'Every morning I walked from the lodgings at Montague Place, reached my consulting room at ten and sat there until three or four with never a ring to disturb my serenity.' His idle time was spent writing detective stories and he was hoping that the meeting would enable him to lead a life as a full-time writer. His name was Arthur Conan Doyle and, despite wearing his best clothes, he was described as looking, at the meeting with Wilde and Stoddart, like 'a walrus in Sunday clothes'. The contrast with the flamboyant Wilde must have been marked. Both writers received generous commissions from Stoddart. Wilde wrote *The Picture of Dorian Gray* which, though successful, was denounced by many critics as immoral and foreshadowed his later fall from grace. Conan Doyle wrote *The Sign of Four*, which marked a major advance in his public reputation and helped to make Sherlock Holmes the world's most celebrated detective. Perhaps out of gratitude, he set some scenes from the story, and from *A Scandal in Bohemia*, in the hotel. The hotel, extensively refurbished, has been popular with such visitors as Winston Churchill, Noel Coward, Wallis Simpson and Charles de Gaulle, and since April 2009 has borne a green plaque at first-floor level on its eastern wall commemorating the meeting of Oscar Wilde and Conan Doyle at an important point in their respective careers.

PADDINGTON

Paddington is a more mixed area socially than are the grander parts of the City of Westminster, but its place in children's literature is assured since it gave its name to Paddington Bear, who appeared at Paddington station in 1958, having arrived from 'darkest Peru' by some unspecified means of transport. His rather shabby appearance, with an old suitcase and a duffel coat, together with his taste for marmalade sandwiches, has helped to make him an object of affection to children throughout the world, who can read of his exploits in thirty languages. He is the creation of Michael Bond, who first conceived the idea when he saw a bear in a shop near Paddington station and bought it for his wife for Christmas 1956. The first story, *A Bear Called Paddington*, followed in 1958 and tells how the bear was discovered by the Brown family at Paddington station, with a note attached to his coat which read 'Please look after this bear'. Bond recalled evacuee children at railway stations during the war with similar labels attached to their clothes. The Browns take him to their home in Windsor Gardens, Maida Vale, and feed him marmalade sandwiches. Similar stories have followed over the subsequent half century. A bronze statue of him at Paddington station is located at the foot of the escalators leading up to the food court, where he was supposedly found.

In 1953 Sir John Betjeman, himself a devotee of teddy bears, set out how the Paddington area had changed since the days when the impeccably middle class Whiteley's, London's first department store, set the tone for the area:

> Through those broad streets to Whiteley's once
> The carriages would pass,
> When ever-weeping Paddington
> Was safely middle class.
> That silent land of stable smells,

High walls and flowering trees,
Is now rack-rented into flats
For busy refugees.

At the time John Betjeman wrote those lines, Paddington, and neighbouring Notting Hill, were being exploited to house West Indian immigrants in poor conditions by landlords like the late Peter Rachman, who gave the word 'Rachmanism' to the language to describe such practices. The areas have since been invaded by bankers, media folk and other plutocrats so that they have now become gentrified and unaffordable to most citizens.

THE STRAND, CHARING CROSS AND WESTMINSTER

South of the Strand are streets and buildings which remind us that in earlier centuries this was the site of grand aristocratic palaces whose gardens, before the construction of the Victoria Embankment, opened on to the Thames. The Savoy was the home of John of Gaunt. Northumberland House, the home of the Dukes of Northumberland, survived until the 1870s and was demolished by Sir Joseph Bazalgette to create a new thoroughfare from Trafalgar Square to the Embankment, now Northumberland Avenue. And Essex Street, the home of the Earl of Essex, earned its imprudent owner a place in history in 1601 when the young earl, Robert Devereux, organised a performance of Shakespeare's *Richard II*, which features the deposition of the king. Essex then attempted to raise a rebellion against Queen Elizabeth I, of whom he had previously been a favourite. She kept her head and he lost his.

Essex Street was also the place where Pip, in *Great Expectations*, found lodgings for Magwitch under the name Provis.

Buckingham Street, formerly the home of the Dukes of Buckingham, now runs from the Strand to Victoria Embankment Gardens and was where Charles Dickens briefly lodged, at No. 15, and where he later lodged his alter ago, David Copperfield, with Mrs Crupp. The building has since been demolished and replaced by a new building overlooking the gardens. Dickens was not the only distinguished resident of No. 15 as it had been for a time the home of Tsar Peter the Great during his visit to London in 1698, and of Henry Fielding in 1735.

Nearby, at No. 142 The Strand (now No. 2 Arundel Street), were the original offices of Dickens's publishers Chapman and Hall who, following the success of *The Pickwick Papers*, received a visit from the author's father, John Dickens, to ask for a loan! John Chapman also published the works of Thomas Carlyle, George Eliot and T.H. Huxley ('Charles Darwin's Bulldog').

Victoria Embankment Gardens was created by Sir Joseph Bazalgette in the 1870s when he built the Victoria Embankment. William Gladstone (1809–98), Prime Minister at the time, wanted to build offices on this rare green space (using the rents to abolish income tax!), but was prevented from doing so by a campaign led by W.H. Smith (1825–91) who, besides running the family business, was MP for Westminster. Apart from the fact that his station bookstalls encouraged many travellers to buy and read books, he occupies a place in our artistic heritage as the model for 'Sir Joseph Porter the Ruler of the Queen's Naveee' in Gilbert and Sullivan's *HMS Pinafore*. Though lampooned, he was in fact a very effective First Lord of the Admiralty, shaking up many archaic practices and people.

The Golden Cross Hotel at Charing Cross, which was demolished when Trafalgar square was created, accommodated Samuel Pickwick and his companions as they began their travels, and also David Copperfield, who encountered Daniel Peggotty in a state of distress on the steps of the nearby church of St Martin-in-the-Fields as Peggotty searched for Little Em'ly who had run away with the villainous Steerforth. David took Peggotty back to the hotel in an attempt to comfort him and eventually located Little Em'ly at a house off Golden Square, Soho.

Charing Cross station occupies the former site of Hungerford fruit and vegetable market, which was demolished to make way for the station in 1862. Hungerford Stairs, nearby, was the home of Warren's Blacking Warehouse, where Charles Dickens worked as a child while his parents were in the Marshalsea debtors' prison for four months in 1824, a short period which left a lifelong scar of shame on the novelist. There the 12-year-old Dickens walked each day from his lodgings in Little College Street (now College Place), Camden Town, along the Hampstead Road, Tottenham Court Road and St Martin's Lane to his place of work. Many years later, the author's son Henry remembered him playing a memory game in which Dickens's clue was 'Warren's Blacking, 30 Strand' where he covered pots of boot blacking 'first with a piece of oil paper, and then with a piece of blue paper'. Hungerford Stairs was also the location at which Mr Micawber, in *David Copperfield*, took ship for a more prosperous life as a colonial magistrate in Australia, freed at last from his endless debts.

Charing Cross station itself was the scene of Ford Madox Ford's poem 'Antwerp', written in the early days of the First World War as an anxious crowd awaits the return of a train carrying troops, including the wounded:

> This is Charing Cross,
> It is midnight;
> There is a great crowd
> And no light.

At the bottom of Whitehall, which runs south from Trafalgar Square, is Parliament Street where Charles Dickens, during his days in the blacking factory, took a glass of ale at the Red Lion, where it was 'served to him with kindness'. David Copperfield does the same. The Red Lion still stands, still serving glasses of ale to those in search of Dickens, and to MPs and journalists from the Palace of Westminster nearby.

A short walk across Parliament Square into St Margaret Street and Millbank takes us to Dean Stanley Street and Smith Square. Here Jenny Wren, the crippled dolls' dressmaker, lived with her drunken father in *Our Mutual Friend*. Smith Square, dominated by St John's church, is now a very grand place indeed, but in Dickens's time it was not so, and Jenny Wren's house, in the shadow of the great baroque church, has 'deadly repose on it, more as though it had taken laudanum than fallen

The world famous Piccadilly Circus as seen in 1932. (Wikimedia Commons)

into a natural rest'. Jenny described the huge church, now used mostly for concerts, as 'generally resembling some petrified monster, frightened and gigantic, on its back with its legs in the air'.

PICCADILLY AND SOHO

Piccadilly itself was lampooned as a thoroughfare for the pretentious in the operetta *Patience*, which is a satire on the posturing of aesthetes, particularly Oscar Wilde. It was the sixth work of Gilbert and Sullivan and contains the phrase 'As I walk down Piccadilly with a poppy or a lily in my mediaeval hand'. Oscar Wilde also expressed strong views about the artists' models, who were to be found in London in the late nineteenth century and were to be seen in the bohemian quarters around Soho and Piccadilly. He described them as 'Intellectual Philistines' and declared that: 'For an artist to marry his model is as fatal as for a gourmet to marry his cook: the one gets no sittings and the other gets no dinners.'

The Criterion Bar at the east end of Piccadilly, near the Eros statue, was the place where Dr Watson, anxiously seeking affordable accommodation, was told by his young friend Stamford of 'a fellow who is working at the chemical laboratory up at the hospital' looking to share with someone. When Watson expressed interest he was warned: 'You don't know Sherlock Holmes yet, perhaps you would not care for him as a constant companion.' Thus began one of the most famous partnerships in literary history.

Indeed, it was outside the Cafe Royal restaurant, once a grand old restaurant at the Piccadilly end of Regent Street, that Holmes was viciously attacked in *The Adventure of the Illustrious Client*.

No. 347 Piccadilly was the house that Count Dracula purchased in Bram Stoker's novel. Although the address doesn't

The Cafe Royal restaurant on Regent Street shortly after its closure in 2008. (Mark Beynon)

No. 138 Piccadilly is believed to have been the building Bram Stoker based Count Dracula's London residence on. It is now home to Eon Productions, the company behind the James Bond films. (Meyer Verlag)

exist, contemporary writers have suggested 138 Piccadilly was the building Stoker had in mind when he wrote the novel.

John Galsworthy, in the second volume of *The Forsyte Saga*, entitled *In Chancery*, wrote that:

> Soho is least suited to the Forsyte spirit. Untidy, full of Greeks, Ishmaelites, cats, Italians, tomatoes, restaurants, organs, coloured stuffs, queer names, people looking out of upper windows, it dwells remote from the British Body Politic. Yet has it haphazard proprietary instincts of its own, and a certain possessive prosperity which keeps its rents up when those of other quarters go down.

Adam Dalgleish, P.D. James's poetry-writing detective, described Soho in *Unnatural Causes* (1967) as: 'An agreeable place to dine; a cosmopolitan village tucked away behind Piccadilly with its own mysterious village life, one of the best shopping centres for food in London, the nastiest and most sordid nursery of crime in Europe.'

Robert Westerby's (1909–68) 1937 novel *Wide Boys Never Work* was an account of the Soho criminal underworld and introduced the expression 'wide boy' to the language to describe a dishonest person on the fringes of crime. The book was made into a film, *Soho Incident*, in 1956 and republished in 2008. These descriptions of Soho are recognisable today, though rents are no doubt supported by the large number of media organisations – magazines, television producers and film companies – who have made it their home.

In Wardour Street, Soho, stands the tower of St Anne's Church, all that remains of a church built in the late seventeenth century to a design by Christopher Wren; the rest of the building was destroyed in a bombing raid in 1940. In 1976 an appeal to restore the tower was launched by John Betjeman, who wrote some lines for the occasion:

High in the air two barrels interlock
To form the faces of this famous clock
Reduced to drawing-room size this clock would be
A Paris ornament of 1803.
Let's make it go again, let London know
That life and heart and hope are in Soho.

Not, perhaps, his most memorable lines, but the tower, and eventually the whole church, was rebuilt.

Nearby, at No. 43 Gerrard Street, is the former site of the infamous '43 Club', run by Mrs Kate Meyrick in the intervals between her spells in jail for offences ranging from selling alcohol without a licence to bribing the police. It was very popular with artists and writers, and makes many appearances in novels featuring the 'Bright Young People'. In Anthony Powell's *Dance to the Music of Time* it is the haunt of the drunkard Charles Stringham, and in *Brideshead Revisited* it is the club to which Charles Ryder, Sebastian Flyte and 'Boy' Mulcaster retreat, following which Sebastian is arrested for driving while drunk. The latter event was based on an incident when Matthew Ponsonby (brother of Elizabeth, see page 101) was fined £20 for driving in the Strand while drunk, his father attributing this misdemeanour to the influence of the 'disreputable friend' with whom he was driving – Evelyn Waugh!

In *Bleak House* Esther Summerson, the unacknowledged daughter of Lady Dedlock, meets Caroline ('Caddy') Jellyby in Soho Square, and to the south of the square is Manette Street, linking Greek Street to Charing Cross Road, which reminds us that this was the home of Dr Manette after his release from the Bastille in *A Tale of Two Cities*. To the west is Golden Square, where Dickens places the grand home of Ralph Nickleby, though many of the houses that existed in Dickens's time, including No. 13 which has been suggested as Ralph's, have been demolished. Dickens disparages the square, informing the reader in *Nicholas Nickleby* that:

Brown's Hotel on Albemarle Street was the inspiration for Agatha Christie's Bertram's Hotel. (Mark Beynon)

> It is one of the squares that have been; a quarter of the town that has gone down in the world and has taken to letting lodgings. Many of its first and second floors are let, furnished, to single gentlemen; and it takes boarders besides. It is a great resort of foreigners. The dark-complexioned men who wear large rings, and heavy watch-guards, and bushy whiskers, and who congregate under the Opera Colonnade, and about the box-office in the season, between four and five in the afternoon… Its boarding houses are musical and the notes of pianos and harps float in the evening time round the head of the mournful statue, the guardian genius of the little wilderness of shrubs in the centre of the square.

One of the square's more humble dwellings also serves for a time as a refuge for Little Em'ly after she is found by Martha Endell after Em'ly's abandonment by the villainous Steerforth in *David Copperfield*. The square is now the home of companies in the advertising, entertainment and fashion businesses, but its nineteenth-century buildings are still in evidence.

Cambridge Circus, an intersection of Shaftesbury Avenue and Charing Cross Road, is the home of John Le Carré's fictional headquarters of the British intelligence service in his George Smiley novels. Aptly nicknamed 'The Circus', the headquarters is believed by some to have occupied 90 Charing Cross Road, just north of Cambridge Circus.

MAYFAIR AND ST JAMES'S

The Mayfair district of London, usually associated with the final (and most expensive) stop on the Monopoly board, is bounded by Park Lane, Regent Street, Oxford Street and Piccadilly. It takes its name from a fair held in May near Hyde

Park Corner until 1764, but didn't assume a clear identity until the architect John Nash (1752–1835) constructed its eastern boundary, Regent Street, to separate it from Soho, in 1813–16. Much of it belongs to the Grosvenor family, later Dukes of Westminster, whose judicious marriages (for example in 1677 to Mary Davies, who brought to the estate the land now occupied by Davies Street and much else besides) created a property empire of unsurpassed value. It has long been associated with wealth and aristocracy, and benefits from its proximity to the even more exclusive St James's district to the south of Piccadilly with its royal palaces and gentlemen's clubs. This takes its name from St James's Palace, a former leper hospital which was taken over by Henry VIII and turned into a fine Tudor palace and royal residence. Foreign ambassadors are still accredited to the Court of St James and the palace is at present the London home of Princess Anne, the Princess Royal.

On Albemarle Street lies the upmarket Brown's Hotel, considered to be the inspiration for the setting of Agatha Christie's Miss Marple novel *At Bertram's Hotel*. Arthur Holmwood stays here in *Dracula*, although in the book it is referred to as the Albemarle Hotel. Nearby, to the north, is Mount Street, which contains the London home of Archdeacon Grantly in Anthony Trollope's Barchester novels, and to the west is Bruton Street, which is the London home of the Bishop of Barchester and his wife, the formidable Mrs Proudie (it was also the home of the late Queen Mother as a young woman, from which she proceeded to her marriage to the future George VI and where the future Queen Elizabeth II was born).

A short distance away, across the Mall, stands Buckingham Palace, which has been the London home of the sovereign since the reign of George IV (1820–30). It is the subject of one of A.A. Milne's best-known 'Christopher Robin' poems, 'Buckingham Palace', which begins:

They're changing guard at Buckingham Palace –
Christopher Robin went down with Alice.
Alice is marrying one of the guard.
'A soldier's life is terribly hard,'
Says Alice.

They're changing guard at Buckingham Palace –
Christopher Robin went down with Alice.
We saw a guard in a sentry-box.
'One of the sergeants looks after their socks,'
Says Alice.

In *Mrs Dalloway* Virginia Woolf made one of her rare excursions from her Bloomsbury redoubt into the fashionable West End (where she had been brought up, at No. 22 Hyde Park Gate) and commented unflatteringly on the architecture of the Palace: 'A child with a box of bricks could have done better.' A similar verdict is delivered by Nazneen, the heroine of Monica Ali's *Brick Lane*, with its not always sympathetic portrayal of the area's Bangladeshi community. After living in London for many years, rarely straying much beyond Brick Lane itself, Nazneen gives her verdict on the monarch's London home:

> If she were Queen she would tear it down and build a new house, not this flat-roofed block but something elegant and spirited, with minarets and spires, domes and mosaics, a beautiful garden instead of this bare forecourt. Something like the Taj Mahal.

EVELYN WAUGH

Mayfair and St James's feature extensively in the works of Evelyn Waugh and P.G. Wodehouse, and to a lesser extent in the works of other authors. Much of Evelyn Waugh's early novel *Vile Bodies* is set in the Mayfair and St James's area. It was made into a film, *Bright Young Things*, by Stephen Fry and many scenes in the novel are set in the Cavendish Hotel, which still flourishes on the corner of Duke Street and Jermyn Street, to the south of Piccadilly. In the novel it is called Shepheard's Hotel. The Cavendish was run by an eccentric proprietress called Rosa Lewis (1867–1952), of whom the novelist (and friend of Waugh) Anthony Powell wrote: 'All Cavendish life completely depended on the proprietress.' Rosa and the hotel featured in a television series of the 1970s called *The Duchess of Duke Street*.

Rosa was a watchmaker's daughter who became cook to Lady Randolph Churchill (Winston's mother). With her husband, a butler called Excelsior Lewis, she took a house in Eaton Terrace, Belgravia, which she seems to have run as a bordello for the particular convenience of King Edward VII, who may have helped her to buy the Cavendish Hotel, which she ran from 1904–52. In 1914, following the outbreak of war, she transferred a signed photograph of the Kaiser from the drawing room to the servants' lavatory. Aldous Huxley, who often used the hotel, described it as 'a run-down country house – large, comfortable rooms but everything shabby and a bit dirty'. When the hotel was visited by a famous American pianist, Rosa told him: 'Go and play Old Man River and do as you're told.' The only wine served was champagne, the cost being put on the bill of whoever seemed most likely to be able to afford it. Rosa was noted for her inconsequential conversations. One resident was greeted as follows:

Rosa: 'Have you come about the drains?'
Resident: 'I'm staying here.'
Rosa: 'Then why are you wearing a brown hat?'

Such a character was irresistible to Evelyn Waugh, who presented Rosa as Lottie Crump, proprietress of Shepheard's Hotel, in *Vile Bodies* with many of Rosa's habits, including that of charging food and drink to any guest who was wealthy or had offended her. In *Vile Bodies* this role is assigned to 'Judge Thingummy', an American judge whose anxiety to ingratiate himself with the assembled company makes him an easy victim of Lottie's vicarious generosity. In an article in the *Daily Mail* in May 1930 entitled 'People who want to sue me', Evelyn Waugh disavowed any intention of portraying Rosa as Lottie Crump. He wrote:

> I made it the most fantastic hotel I could devise. I filled it with an impossible clientele. I invented an impossible proprietress. I gave it a fictitious address. I described its management as so eccentric and incompetent that no hotel could be run on their lines for a week without coming into the police or bankruptcy court. Here at last I thought I was safely in the realm of pure imagination.

Rosa, however, was not deceived. After *Vile Bodies* was published she declared: 'There are two bastards I'm not going to have in this house. One is that rotten little Donegal [a gossip columnist of the time] and the other is that swine Evelyn Waugh.' Waugh recalled that the last words she ever spoke to him were 'Take your arse out of my chair'. In fact, the unmistakeable resemblance of Shepheard's Hotel to the Cavendish was very good publicity and led to its being patronised both by penniless authors and rich Americans, the latter being especially welcomed by Rosa.

In a preface to a new edition of *Vile Bodies*, written in 1965 a year before his death, Evelyn Waugh confessed all, writing of Shepheard's Hotel that it was 'A pretty accurate description of Mrs Rosa Lewis and her Cavendish Hotel, just on the brink of their decline but still famous'. Following the death of Rosa Lewis in 1952 the Cavendish was taken in hand by Brian Franks, a professional hotelier friend of Evelyn Waugh, and it is largely his hotel which visitors may now use, secure in the knowledge that they will not be asked to clear the drains and that other people's drinks will not be placed on their bills at the whim of the management!

Another character who appears in *Vile Bodies* is the gossip columnist Mr Chatterbox, who fills his column in the *Daily Excess* with purely imaginary stories about the Bright Young People, including the fact that 'the buffet at Sloane Square tube station had become the haunt of the most modern artistic coterie'.

CLUBLAND

Other parts of the area feature in Evelyn Waugh's works. In Waugh's early wartime work, *Put Out More Flags*, the principal characters have homes in Mayfair, with the alcoholic Angela Lyne living in 'a set of five large rooms high up in the mansard floor of a brand new block in Grosvenor Square'.

The St James's area is also the home of Bellamy's Club, where Guy Crouchback spends much of his time in the war trilogy *Sword of Honour* as Waugh himself did in its original, White's Club, during his frequent visits to London. White's Club, at the top of St James's Street, dates from 1693 and owes its name to its Italian founder, Francesco Bianco (Francis White) who founded it in 1693. It moved to its present site in 1755 and the bay window which is a prominent feature of the building was favoured by one of its members, the dandy Beau Brummell, as a place from which to see and, above all, to be seen. Waugh was for many years a member of Bellamy's/White's. One of London's most exclusive gentlemen's clubs, he used it during his frequent visits to London where it was the scene of many of his drunken rows with fellow members like his friend and wartime companion Randolph Churchill.

This part of London is thick with clubs. Brooks's Club is just across St James's Street and was frequented by Phineas Finn in Anthony Trollope's Palliser novels, as was the Reform Club round the corner in Pall Mall.

No. 33a St James's Street has a curious connection with Conan Doyle. The author, an active sportsman, had become friendly with a well-known strongman and music-hall performer called Eugen Sandow and attended Sandow's Institute of Physical Culture at that address. In 1904 the author was involved in an accident which resulted in his being trapped underneath his car and he attributed his survival to the muscular development he had achieved under Sandow's direction.

No. 28 Northumberland Avenue was the Constitutional Club where Conan Doyle sometimes lunched with his fellow member P.G. Wodehouse. In 1959 it moved to Pall Mall and closed in 1979. It appears in a number of Wodehouse novels as 'the Senior Conservative Club' and was, according to *Psmith in the City*, noted for the 'Curiously Gorganzolaesque marble of its main staircase'.

Ian Fleming, creator of James Bond, was a member of Boodle's Club in St James's Street and used it as a model for Blades Club, of which 'M' was a member, Bond being taken there by him as a guest. Fleming borrowed the name of a fellow member for one of his arch-villains: Blofeld. There is a reference to the club in Oscar Wilde's play of 1895, *An Ideal Husband*, when it is said of a bachelor peer 'Lord Goring is the result of Boodle's Club'. In *Bleak House* Dickens, in a reference to the incestuous way in which political power and influence is passed to and fro between small clubbish groups, writes of Lords Boodle and Coodle, Sir Thomas Doodle and the Duke of Foodle.

Perhaps the oddest fictional club was that of Sherlock Holmes's cleverer brother Mycroft. He belonged to the Diogenes Club, Pall Mall, where 'no member is permitted to take the least notice of any other one'.

Further down St James's Street, at No. 87, was the St James's Coffee House where Joseph Addison wrote many of the early editions of *The Spectator*, founded as a daily publication in 1711 with the declared desire 'to enliven morality with wit, and to temper wit with morality … to bring philosophy out of the closets and libraries, schools and colleges, to dwell in clubs and assemblies, at tea-tables and coffeehouses'.

Nearby is 'Marchmain House', St James's Street, London home of the Flyte family in Evelyn Waugh's *Brideshead Revisited* which, converted into flats, becomes the headquarters of Hazardous Offensive Operations, one of the many units to which Guy Crouchback is seconded during his motley military career in Waugh's great wartime trilogy *Sword of Honour*. Marchmain House does not exist but may be identified with any of the grand aristocratic houses which border Green Park and the Mall. The exterior of Bridgewater House in Cleveland Row which, like Marchmain House, backs on to Green Park, was used as Marchmain House for the 1981 Granada TV version of *Brideshead Revisited*.

BRIGHT YOUNG PEOPLE

Across Piccadilly from Green Park, leading from Park Lane towards Berkeley Square, is Curzon Street, once the home of the adventuress Becky Sharp in *Vanity Fair* and later the home of the Duc de Richleau in Dennis Wheatley's bizarre 1934 novel of black magic and the occult, *The Devil Rides Out*. Later made into a 'Hammer' film starring Christopher Lee as the Duke and Charles Gray as Mocata, the evil practitioner of the black arts, it also featured Medina Place, St John's Wood as the home of Simon Arum where the Satanists meet. This has been identified as a cul-de-sac close to Lord's cricket ground, Melina Place, which was once the home of the novelist Anthony Powell, a friend of Wheatley. Simon Arum is rescued from the cult by Richleau, with the assistance of occult knowledge gained from artefacts in the British Museum.

Curzon Street is still the site of Heywood Hill's bookshop, formerly the workplace of the novelist Nancy Mitford. During the time that she worked there, and particularly during the Second World War, the shop became a gathering place for Nancy's well-connected friends and it was while working there that Nancy, unhappily married, met the love of her life in Gaston Palewski, General de Gaulle's right-hand man. In her novel *The Pursuit of Love* her heroine Linda works in a bookshop in a 'slummy little street', a less than adequate description of one of Mayfair's most elegant thoroughfares, but clearly a reference to Nancy's own experience. Linda marries the rather grim banker Tony, but while working in the bookshop she meets her Gaston, Fabrice de Sauveterre, whereupon 'she knew that this was love ... she knew that never before, not even in dreams, and she was a great dreamer of love, had she felt anything remotely like this'. Linda eventually leaves her husband for the Communist sympathiser Christian to live in the then less fashionable Cheyne Walk. The book has many autobiographical elements and reflects the need for Nancy and her friends, who became known as the Bright Young People, to be endlessly amused: 'The worst of being a Communist is that the parties you may go to are, well, awfully funny and touching but not very gay' as Linda tells her sister.

Many of the same characters appear in *Vile Bodies*, the second novel of Nancy's lifelong friend Evelyn Waugh. The Bright Young People are based on a group of wealthy, rootless and directionless individuals with whom Waugh (and Nancy Mitford) were loosely and sometimes uncomfortably associated. In a foreword to the novel on its publication Waugh wrote: 'Bright Young People and others kindly note that all characters are entirely imaginary (and you get far too much publicity already, whoever you are).' This is disingenuous since it is not hard to put names to many of the principal characters in the book, notably the 'heroine' Agatha Runcible who was amongst those who 'all got into taxicabs and drove across Berkeley Square' in the heart of Mayfair, heading for the home of Miss Brown, who fervently wishes to be adopted by the Bright Young People as one of their number. The Bright Young People have attended a Hawaiian party and are dressed accordingly. Miss Brown takes them to her home, feeds them and is overcome with excitement when Agatha Runcible, clad in the Hawaiian costume that was *de rigeur*, asks to stay the night. The following morning Agatha, having burst in upon 'a sweet old boy sitting at a desk' (the Prime Minister) finally realises where she is, at 10 Downing Street, and, 'trailing garlands of equatorial flowers, fled out of the room and out of the house to the huge delight and profit of the crowd of reporters and press photographers who were already massed round the historic front door'. In due course 'Midnight orgies at No.10' are reported and the government falls.

Cruttwell makes a further appearance, though this time he has fallen in rank and, as Captain Cruttwell MP, receives a petition from the Ladies' Conservative Association of Chesham Bois, calling upon him to withdraw his support for the prime minister. Agatha Runcible is regarded by many as a fanciful representation of Elizabeth Ponsonby, the daughter of a cabinet minister and granddaughter of the composer Sir Hubert Parry. After a dissipated life she died, still a young woman, of alcoholic poisoning.

Hyde Park Corner was the site of another of the Bright Young People's escapades where, after attending a 'Mozart Party' in eighteenth-century costume, the revellers joined a group of workmen repairing gas mains there, a photograph of the incongruous event duly appearing in the press. The Downing Street episode in *Vile Bodies* also owes something to an event in the life of the Lygon family, who are identified with the Flytes in *Brideshead Revisited*. Lady Mary and Lady Sibell Lygon returned to the home of their father, Halkin House (the site now occupied by the Halkin Hotel in Halkin Street, Belgravia), to find themselves locked out and walked instead to Downing Street, the home of their friends the Baldwins, to request a bed for the night.

The atmosphere of parties in Belgravia like the one which ended with bewildered employees of the gas company at Hyde Park Gate is well conveyed in *Vile Bodies* as the Bright Young People arrive at a party to welcome an American Evangelist, Mrs Melrose Ape, a character based upon an American evangelist called Aimee Semple Macpherson:

> The Bright Young People came popping all together, out of someone's electric brougham like a litter of pigs, and ran squealing up the steps. Some gate-crashers who had made the mistake of coming in Victorian fancy-dress were detected and repulsed. They hurried home to change for a second assault. No-one wanted to miss Mrs Ape's debut.

P.G. Wodehouse's Mayfair was also, of course, the haunt of Bertram ('Bertie') Wilberforce Wooster and those of his friends who frequented the Drones Club, conveniently close to Bertie's flat in Berkeley Street, a refuge for young men with plenty of money and not too much in the way of brains to trouble them. Wodehouse himself briefly occupied a flat at No. 15 Berkeley Street in 1922, which appears in 'Sir Roderick Comes to Lunch' as the flat in which is entertained Sir Roderick Spode, leader of the Blackshorts, a thinly disguised portrait of Oswald Moseley's Blackshirts. Here Bertie would meet such chums as Rupert Psmith, Hildebrand ('Tuppy') Glossop, Oofie Prosser, Bingo Little, Gussie Fink-Nottle and Fergy Fungie-Phipps, Bertie informing his numerous ferocious aunts that he is attending a meeting of the club's Fine Arts Committee. Since women were in no circumstances admitted to the Drones, except as waitresses or cleaners, there was no danger of Bertie's subterfuges being exposed even though the dreaded Aunt Dahlia had a flat nearby.

Evelyn Waugh, a dedicated clubman himself and a great admirer of P.G. Wodehouse, claimed that the Drones Club resembled no club that had ever existed or could possibly exist, but other commentators have traced its origins to three Mayfair clubs which flourished from about the turn of the nineteenth/twentieth century. The first was the Bachelors' Club at 106 Piccadilly which, as its name implies, was for men determined to avoid the pitfalls of marriage, as Bertie Wooster certainly was. Field Marshal Kitchener was amongst the more eminent members of the Bachelors' Club before it was replaced by Buck's Club, which took its name from its founder Herbert Buckmaster, first husband of the actress Gladys Cooper. Buckmaster and a group of fellow officers who had fought in the First World War founded the club specifically for younger people whose spirits needed to be raised after their ordeals in the trenches, so it could be said to have foreshadowed the activities of the Bright Young People whom Evelyn Waugh satirised and who abandoned themselves to light-hearted pleasure. Wodehouse never became a member of Buck's Club, but frequently lunched there as a guest and he makes several references to Buck's Club in his works. He gave the name McGarry to the barman of the fictional Drones Club, this being the name of the real barman of Buck's Club who in 1921 created Bucks Fizz, a mixture of Champagne and orange juice, which often brought relief to Bertie Wooster and other Drones after a heavy night out. Winston Churchill was a member of Buck's Club. At the beginning of *Eggs, Beans and Crumpets*, Wodehouse's description of the Drones Club clearly has in mind the real home of Buck's Club as it exists today at its original home at No. 18 Clifford Street, Mayfair:

> In the heart of London's clubland there stands a tall and grimly forbidding edifice known to taxi drivers and the elegant young men who frequent its precincts as the Drones Club. Yet its somewhat austere exterior belies the atmosphere of cheerful optimism and bonhomie that lies within.

At the end of Clifford Street are Grafton Street and Bond Street, the site of the famous jewellers Asprey's which appears as Aspinalls in many Wodehouse works. A third influence on the Drones was the Bath Club which, like the Drones, had a swimming pool in which members were occasionally immersed. It was based at 34 Dover Street from its foundation in 1894 until 1941, when it was destroyed in the Blitz, following which it found temporary homes before closing in 1981. This was the original of the club into whose pool Tuppy Glossop propelled Bertie Wooster 'in the full soup and fish' (i.e. full evening dress).

And let us not forget Reginald Jeeves, himself a member of the Junior Ganymede Club for 'Gentlemen's Gentlemen', located in a public house on the corner of Hay's Mews and Charles Street and going by the improbable name 'The Only Running Footman', a reference to the eighteenth-century practice of having a footman running ahead of a gentleman's carriage. In the Junior Ganymede Club the gentlemen's gentlemen recorded their observations on their employers, eleven pages of the book, according to Jeeves, being devoted to the activities of Bertie Wooster. The pub was built in 1749 and rebuilt in the 1930s.

Nearby to the south, at 110a Piccadilly, was the home of Lord Peter Wimsey, the fictional detective created by Dorothy L. Sayers, the site now occupied by the Park Lane Hotel. The addition of the 'a' to the address is thought by some to be a slightly cheeky reference to the 'b' added to 221 by Conan Doyle for his equally fictitious address for the more famous Sherlock Holmes.

Nearby is The Albany, one of London's most exclusive addresses, which was the home of Raffles, the gentleman thief created by E.W. Hornung, brother-in-law of Conan Doyle. Raffles's prowess at cricket earn him invitations to country houses from which he steals to earn a living.

The Only Running Footman in Mayfair is believed to have been the inspiration for the Junior Ganymede Club in P.G. Wodehouse's *Jeeves and Wooster* stories. (Mark Beynon)

CIRCUMLOCUTION IN MAYFAIR

Dickens also places some of his characters in the heart of Mayfair. Mr Tite Barnacle of the Circumlocution Office in *Little Dorrit*, who, in Dickens's words, 'had only one idea in his head and that was a wrong one', bolsters his self-esteem by living in an airless house 'not absolutely in Grosvenor Square itself but it was very near it'. When he has come into his fortune Mr Dorrit, released from the Marshalsea, moves into a hotel in Brook Street.

At the time that Dickens was writing *Little Dorrit*, Mr and Mrs Claridge had just opened their hotel in Brook Street after buying an adjoining property. It is certainly the hotel used by Guy Crouchback in Evelyn Waugh's *Men at Arms*, in an unsuccessful and ultimately humiliating attempt to seduce his former wife, Virginia, though he eventually, and gallantly, remarries her when, destitute, she becomes pregnant by another man. Perhaps Dickens had in mind this hotel, which would become London's grandest, for Old Dorrit.

In Brook Street Dorrit is visited by the crooked financier Merdle, a resident of Harley Street on the slightly less fashionable north side of Oxford Street. Merdle later commits suicide after his bank collapses, taking with it Dorrit's fortune. Merdle's fate owed much to the example of the fraudster John Sadlier of the Tipperary Bank who, in 1856, committed suicide on Hampstead Heath by swallowing prussic acid. *Little Dorrit* was completed the following year.

'A GREAT DEBAUCHEE'

The St James's district, across Piccadilly, was not for Bertie Wooster since the gentlemen's clubs frequented by Evelyn Waugh like White's (Brown's in *Uneasy Money*) were too staid for young men who, when they wanted attention from a club servant would 'heave a bit of bread at him'. Nor did Wooster consider becoming a candidate for the Athenaeum, a haunt of intellectuals and prelates which appears in

Something Fishy and *Money in the Bank* as Lord Uffenham's club The Mausoleum.

Nearby, in what is perhaps the grandest street in this, the grandest part of London, is Carlton House Terrace, which overlooks the Mall and is the London home of the old Duke of Omnium, a prominent character in the Palliser novels, though Trollope's verdict on him is most clearly expressed in his novel *Dr Thorne*:

> He rarely went near the presence of majesty, and when he did so, he did it merely as a disagreeable duty incident to his position … the Queen might be queen so long as he was the Duke of Omnium. Their revenues were about the same, with the exception that the duke's were his own … In person he was a plain, thin man, tall, but undistinguished in appearance, except that there was a gleam of pride in his eye which seemed every moment to be saying 'I am the Duke of Omnium.' He was unmarried, and, if report said true, a great debauchee.

To the north of Carlton House Terrace is Suffolk Street which was once the location of Anthony Trollope's favourite London hotel, Garlant's. He chose it for Eleanor, the daughter of the Revd Septimus Harding, as a convenient place to stay in London after she had married the innocuous clergyman the Revd Francis Arabin in *Barchester Towers*, and Trollope himself lived there for the last year of his life, suffering a stroke in November 1882 and dying the following month.

POST OFFICES AND PRINCES

Anthony Trollope was long employed by the Post Office and is credited with the invention of the pillar box. One of his places of work was the headquarters of the Post Office at St Martin's le Grand, off Newgate Street. Until 1697 criminals could seek sanctuary in the grounds of the monastery, and later college, of St Martin's le Grand. Sir Thomas More, in a work of 1513, claimed that Miles Forrest, one of those accused of murdering the Princes in the Tower, 'rotted away piecemeal' in the sanctuary.

Anthony Trollope, more often associated with the cloisters of Barchester, showed a familiarity with London's social gradations in many of his novels. Madame Max Goesler, the wealthy widow who befriends, rescues from conviction and finally marries Phineas Finn, the principal character in two of the Palliser novels, has a house in Park Lane, while Trollope places the crooked financier Melmotte, in *The Way We Live Now*, in a house in Grosvenor Square, the heart of Mayfair, though his downfall and suicide follow. Grosvenor Place, nearby, is the London home of Lady Laura Standish in *Phineas Finn* following her marriage to the immensely wealthy but obsessive and jealous Mr Kennedy. Convinced that Phineas Finn is the cause of his wife's discontent, Kennedy tries to shoot Finn in a hotel in Judd Street, which runs south of the Euston Road opposite St Pancras station. Kennedy then sinks into madness and dies. In *The Prime Minister* the barely reputable Lady Eustace lived in 'a very small house bordering upon Mayfair but the street, though very small, and having disagreeable relation with a mews, still had an air of fashion about it'. Trollope shows a more subtle touch in *The Small House at Allington* when Lady Alexandrina de Courcy nearly makes the 'fatal error' of moving to Pimlico, the more modest neighbour of the grander Belgravia. She raises her sights accordingly towards Eaton Square in the heart of Belgravia: 'if indeed they could have achieved Eaton Square … her geographical knowledge of Pimlico had not been perfect and she had very nearly fallen into a fatal error.'

BELGRAVIA

South-west of Mayfair, to the south of Hyde Park, are the Belgravia and Pimlico districts. Like Bloomsbury, these were created by the builder Thomas Cubitt (1788–1855) in the early nineteenth century on marshy land which, in this case, belonged mostly to the Grosvenor family, who also own much of Mayfair. The area is bounded to the north and south by Hyde Park and the Thames; and to the east and west by Buckingham Palace Road and Sloane Street. As in Mayfair itself the family's names and properties are reflected in names of streets and other features of the area. Belgravia itself takes its name from one of the family's properties at Belgrave in Leicestershire; Eaton Square is named after Eaton Hall, the Grosvenor country home in Cheshire; and Lupus Street, in Pimlico, remembers Lupus Grosvenor, 1st Duke of Westminster (1825–99). Belgravia, from an early date, was a very fashionable area owing to its proximity to Buckingham Palace. It is now the home of many embassies and Joseph Conrad, in his novel *The Secret Agent*, places the Russian Embassy there in the 1880s, his double agent Verloc, spy, agent provocateur and pornographer walking from his premises in Soho to the embassy via Rotten Row in Hyde Park.

Belgravia quickly acquired a reputation for affluence, not always accompanied by generosity, as reflected in Matthew Arnold's poem 'West London':

Crouched on the pavement, close by Belgrave Square,
A tramp I saw, ill, moody and tongue-tied.
A babe was in her arms, and at her side
A girl, their clothes were rags, their feet were bare.

Some labouring men, whose work lay somewhere there,
Passed opposite; she touched the girl, who hied
Across, and begged, and came back satisfied.
The rich she had let pass, with frozen stare.

Thought I 'Above her state this spirit towers;
She will not ask of aliens, but of friends,
Of sharers in a common human fate'.

Platform 9¾ at King's Cross station, made famous by the *Harry Potter* stories. (Lauren Manning)

6

CAMDEN AND ISLINGTON

The London boroughs of Camden and Islington contain many places which are rich in literary associations. John Keats's home in Keats Grove, Hampstead is now a museum to the poet's memory, while the Bloomsbury squares which are strongly associated with Virginia Woolf, Lytton Strachey and others retain much of the tranquillity which attracted members of that oddly fascinating and self-absorbed group of friends, though it is doubtful whether they could afford to live there now. Charles Dickens's home in Doughty Street is the only one of his many London homes which survives (and bears a Blue Plaque to mark the fact) and in more recent times King's Cross station has featured prominently in the Harry Potter books and films.

KING'S CROSS STATION

Like John Betjeman, G.K. Chesterton was moved to verse by a railway station in his 1900 poem 'King's Cross Station':

> The circled cosmos whereof man is god
> Has suns and stars of green and gold and red,

And cloudlands of great smoke, that range o-er range
Far floating, hide its iron heavens o-erhead.

God! Shall we ever honour what we are,
And see one moment 'ere the age expire,
The vision of man shouting and erect,
Whirled by the shrieking steeds of flood and fire?

Platform 9¾ at King's Cross is, of course, the point from which the Hogwarts Express departs, carrying Harry Potter and his friends to Hogsmeade station and their destination at Hogwarts boarding school where young wizards and witches are taught magic by Albus Dumbledore and others. Hogwarts itself is somewhere in Scotland, a destination served from King's Cross by the *Flying Scotsman* as well as by J.K. Rowling's mythical train. In an interview J.K. Rowling admitted that she confused the platform layout at King's Cross with that of Euston when writing her books, so King's Cross gained an unintended distinction. King's Cross station was in fact used in filming some of the Harry Potter movies, as was Goathland on the North Yorkshire Moors Railway, which runs steam trains of the kind that have long been absent from King's Cross itself. When filming at King's Cross, a notice was placed on the ground outside platforms 9 and 10 pointing to the Hogwarts Express. It was later removed and a 'Platform 9¾' sign was erected on a wall of the real platforms 9 and 10.

CLERKENWELL

Dickens placed much of the action in *Oliver Twist* in the Clerkenwell area, describing in detail the route taken in the novel by the Artful Dodger as he leads Oliver to Fagin's den in Saffron Hill (then a disreputable quarter) where Fagin awaits Oliver. Much of the route the two boys follow may easily be followed on a map today:

> They crossed from the Angel into St John's road; struck down the small street which terminates at Sadler's Wells Theatre; through Exmouth Street and Coppice Row … thence into Little Saffron Hill and so into Saffron Hill the Great; along which the Dodger scuttled at a rapid pace, directing Oliver to follow close at his heels … A dirtier or more wretched place he had never seen … and from several of the doorways great ill-looking fellows were emerging; bound, to all appearance, on no very well-disposed or harmless errands.

As they walked past New River Head, adjacent to Sadler's Wells, they would have passed the residence of Uriah Heep in *David Copperfield*. It is likely that the story of Oliver Twist's association with Fagin and the Artful Dodger arose from a report in *The Times* on 14 January 1834 of the case of Edward Trabshaw, who had run away from a good home after a dispute with his father and been picked up by John Murphy, a boy of about his age, in Regent Street. Murphy took Trabshaw to Murphy's father 'Old Murphy the child stealer' (who had 'a countenance in which cunning and ferocity were strongly blended'), where he joined about a dozen other children in a 'dark and filthy room' in Cross Lane, which was then near Drury Lane. Old Murphy told Trabshaw that he could stay 'provided he did everything he desired him to do', the requirement being that he should bring back sixpence or a shilling every time he left the dwelling. Murphy's den was raided by police and Edward Trabshaw was reunited with his father, Murphy protesting that he took the boy in 'out of pure charity'. Dickens began to write *Oliver Twist* shortly after the case was reported and the similarities between Murphy's activities and Fagin's den of young thieves are striking, though Murphy was evidently of Afro-Caribbean stock while Fagin was portrayed as Jewish. Murphy's fate is unknown but Fagin, of course, paid with his life.

The Museum Tavern on Great Russell Street, the inspiration for the Alpha Inn in the Sherlock Holmes story *The Adventure of the Blue Carbuncle*. (Ewan Munro)

Clerkenwell, which in the nineteenth century was an area of much crime and poverty, is the scene of George Gissing's 1889 novel *The Nether World* which, like Somerset Maugham's 1897 work *Liza of Lambeth*, is concerned with the hopeless lives of the poor. It opens in Clerkenwell Close, where 'every alley is thronged with small industries' as it still does, much of the road having survived development. The themes of the novel are poverty, loveless marriages, jealousy, illness and death with little of the hope for the future, which permeates many of the novels of Dickens.

BLOOMSBURY

Bloomsbury, the area behind the British Museum roughly bounded by Grays Inn Road and Tottenham Court Road to the east and west and by Euston Road and New Oxford Street to the north and south, is most often associated with the Bloomsbury Group of writers and artists who were friends of the family of Sir Leslie Stephen, first author of the *Dictionary of National Biography* and father of Vanessa and Virginia (later Virginia Woolf). Blue Plaques in Gordon Square remind the visitor that, containing as it does the homes of Virginia Stephen and her family (at No. 46) and of Lytton Strachey (No. 51), this was the centre of the group's social activity. The area was developed in the 1820s by the builder Thomas Cubitt (1788–1855), who turned its waterlogged meadows (on the Duke of Bedford's estate) into comfortable houses for middle-class families whose fathers worked in the City. The name 'Bloomsbury' is derived from the manor, or 'bury', of William Belmond, who bought it in the thirteenth century, but its streets and squares reflect the fact that it later passed into the hands of the Dukes of Bedford. So it contains Bedford Square; Russell Square (the Bedford family name); Tavistock Square (the eldest son of the duke is the marquis of Tavistock); and Woburn Square (Woburn Abbey being the duke's home). Charles Dickens moved to 48 Doughty Street nearby, in 1836, and lived there for three years.

On the corner of Great Russell Street, opposite the British Museum, is the Museum Tavern, a grand old pub that lays claim to having been the inspiration for Conan Doyle's Alpha Inn in the Sherlock Holmes story *The Adventure of the Blue Carbuncle*. In the story, the proprietor of the Alpha Inn purchases its festive geese from Breckinridge's stand in Covent Garden. One of the geese has the stolen carbuncle hidden in its crop.

WHAT SHALL WE HAVE FOR DINNER?

In Tavistock Square, Tavistock House (now replaced by the headquarters of the British Medical Association) was for nine years (1851–60) the home of Dickens, where he wrote *Bleak House*, *Little Dorrit*, *Hard Times*, *A Tale of Two Cities* and part of *Great Expectations*. And it was while living here that Catherine, Dickens's neglected wife, wrote one of the first cookery books, *What Shall We Have For Dinner?*, under the name 'Lady Maria Clutterbuck'. It is still in print. It was while living at Tavistock House that Charles and Catherine separated, to her great distress, to make way for Dickens's young mistress, the actress Nelly Ternan. Catherine was virtually exiled to Camden and lived apart from Dickens and their children until the author died in 1870. Catherine lived for another nine years and on her deathbed she handed to her daughter Kate the letters that Charles had written to her, instructing her: 'Give these to the British Museum that the world may know he loved me once.'

Tavistock Square in Bloomsbury was the home of Charles Dickens when he wrote *Bleak House*, *Little Dorrit*, *Hard Times*, *A Tale of Two Cities* and part of *Great Expectations*. (Ewan Munro)

At No. 52 Tavistock Square Leonard and Virginia Woolf lived and ran the Hogarth Press. It had been founded in 1917 to provide congenial, therapeutic work for Virginia Woolf while she was recovering from one of her frequent spells of ill-health and was named after their house in Richmond where it began in 1917. The press moved to Tavistock Square in 1924 and remained there until the outbreak of war in 1939. Their first publication, *Two Stories*, contained a short story by each of them, but besides the novels of Virginia Woolf herself they went on to publish works by E.M. Forster, Katherine Mansfield and, most notably, *The Waste Land* by T.S. Eliot, first published in 1924.

Tavistock Square was also the fictional home of the Cadaver Club, whose members include P.D. James's detective superintendent Adam Dalgleish and other men 'with an interest in murder'.

In Dickens's early short story 'A Bloomsbury Christening', published in 1834 before he moved to Doughty Street, Mr and Mrs Charles Kitterbell live at No. 14 Great Russell Street, now a delicatessen which bears a Blue Plaque to record its place in literature. The 'Bloomsbury Christening' of the title occurs at St George's Church, Hart Street, which has since been renamed Bloomsbury Way. The church's unusual spire is clearly visible in Hogarth's 1750 print *Gin Lane* and in the same year the novelist and magistrate Henry Fielding published his Inquiry into the increase of London robberies and attributed the problem to the increase in gin drinking which had been brought to England earlier in the century by William of Orange. You could be 'drunk for a penny and dead drunk for twopence' at a time when gin carried no duty and was widely used as a sedative for infants, turning them into alcoholics before they were weaned.

Nearby is Great Ormond Street, home of the famous children's hospital which was founded in 1852 and of which Dickens was an enthusiastic supporter, both writing and giving public readings of *A Christmas Carol* to raise funds, the latter activity launching his very successful career of public readings.

It is probably the hospital to which Betty Higden's grandson Johnny is taken to die in Dickens's *Our Mutual Friend*, and the hospital was also supported by J.M. Barrie (1860–1937) who left to the hospital the royalties of *Peter Pan*.

Our Mutual Friend, published in 1865, is the story of John Harmon, who has been committed to marry the shrewish Bella Wilfer under the terms of his wealthy father's will. John conceals his identity on return from abroad to learn something of Bella's character, a deception made easier by the widespread belief that he is dead. Mr and Mrs Boffin, the kindly employees of old Harmon, contrive a series of incidents through which young John Harmon and Bella Wilfer come to appreciate each other's qualities and the two marry. The book contains a number of important minor characters, notably Jenny Wren, the dolls' dressmaker, and Lizzie Hexham, the daughter of a boatman.

FOUNDLINGS AND *VANITY FAIR*

A further link with both authors is to be found in nearby Coram Fields, just to the north of Great Ormond Street. This was the original home of the Thomas Coram Foundation or Foundling Hospital, founded by the sea captain of that name in 1739 as a home for abandoned children. Dickens, whose home in Doughty Street was close by, wrote of it in 1853 that 'This home of the blank [i.e. nameless] children is by no means a blank place … the Governors of this charity are a model to all others'. In *Little Dorrit* the character Tattycoram is a Coram Foundling. At the first performance of *Peter Pan* in 1904 Barrie insisted that children from the Foundling Hospital be in the audience, confident that the laughter of children would have an infectious influence on the audience. The stratagem worked. Coram Fields remains the only park in London which adults may not enter unless accompanied by a child. Dickens also places two of his landladies in the area. In one of his early short stories 'The Boarding House' he places Mrs Tibbs in Great Coram Street:

> The house of Mrs Tibbs was decidedly the neatest in all Great Coram Street, as clean and bright as indefatigable white-washing and hearth-stoning and scrubbing and rubbing could make them. The wonder was that the brass door-plate with the interesting inscription MRS TIBBS had never caught fire from constant friction, so perseveringly was it polished.

Great Coram Street, with its charming Victorian terraces, was demolished in the 1970s to make way for the concrete mass of the Brunswick Centre which lies between Brunswick Square and Marchmont Street, though much of the surrounding area has been preserved, including Dickens's former home in Doughty Street. Another landlady, Mrs Lirriper, in Dickens's early story of that name, was also in Great Coram Street though she soon moved to 81 Norfolk Street, Strand, located, according to her advertisement in *Bradshaw's Railway Guide*, 'mid-way between the City and St James's' where she could charge as much as eighteen shillings a week to the businessmen who were now her clients.

Dickens's contemporary W.M. Thackeray set much of *Vanity Fair* (1847–48) in Bloomsbury which, by the date of the book's publication, had become a well-established residential area for the aspiring middle classes and particularly for those engaged in commerce in the City. Thackeray lived with his family in Coram Street in 1837–43 and his eldest daughter Anne was born there in 1838. In 'The Ballad of Eliza Davis' he wrote:

> Perhaps you know the Foundling chapel,
> Where the little children sing,
> Lord I like to hear on Sunday
> Them there pretty little things.

In *Vanity Fair* Mr Todd lives in Coram Street while the Osborne family, whose great wealth derives from the City, live at No. 96

Russell Square and occupy 'the best pew at the Foundlings [hospital]' through support of which they hope to gain social advancement. Their son, the feckless George Osborne, is disinherited by his ambitious father for marrying Amelia Sedley whose family, also City merchants, live at No. 62 Russell Square but lose their fortune and have to move to the less salubrious Fulham. However, before the family's fall from wealth and grace the innocent Amelia is visited in Russell Square by her penniless and ruthless school friend Becky Sharp, who attempts to charm Amelia's indolent brother Jos, the 'Collector of Boggley Wallah', into marriage, an enterprise in which she fails. Becky manages to maintain a handsome lifestyle with her hopeless husband Rawdon Crawley by becoming the mistress of Lord Steyne, who lives in Gaunt House, an imaginary location which appears to be in the Bloomsbury area. Becky, tired of Rawdon, ensures his death by securing his appointment as governor of fever-ridden Coventry Island.

No. 24 Russell Square was for many years the office of the publisher Faber and Faber, where T.S. Eliot worked as an editor, often making use of the fire escape to exit when warned of the arrival of his wife Vivienne, who was later consigned to a mental hospital where she died. Virginia Woolf, herself no stranger to mental illness, described Vivienne as 'a bag of ferrets' which, she claimed, the poet wore around his neck.

The busybody Lady Southdown in *Vanity Fair* has a home in Brunswick Square, close to the Foundling Hospital, as does Isabella, the sister of Emma in the novel of the same name, which many critics consider to be Jane Austen's finest work. Isabella declares: 'Our part of London is so very superior to most others … the neighbourhood of Brunswick Square is very different from all the rest. We are so very airy. Mr Wingfield thinks the vicinity of Brunswick Square decidedly the most favourable as to air.' At the time this would have been more important than it seems now on account of the 'miasmatic' theory of disease causation. This held that epidemic diseases were transmitted in polluted air (rather than through water or direct contact) so that clean air would have been a major attraction to any prospective householder.

Other more recent literary associations may be found in Gower Street. No. 12 was for many years the home of Lady Ottoline Morrell (1879–1938), whose generous patronage of writers ranging from Lytton Strachey and other members of the Bloomsbury Group to D.H. Lawrence and Aldous Huxley did not spare her from ruthless caricature by those she had helped. In *Women in Love* D.H. Lawrence painted an unflattering portrait of her as Hermione Roddice, a demanding literary hostess, and Aldous Huxley in *Crome Yellow* caused as much offence to Ottoline as Lawrence did with his caricature of literary weekends at Crome, a pastiche of her country home at Garsington Manor in Oxfordshire.

Also in Gower Street is University College, London, where David Lodge was educated, and he set one of his early novels, *The British Museum is Falling Down*, in the area. Further along Gower Street to the south is the University of London Senate House and Library. Opened in 1936 to an art deco design by Charles Holden (who also designed many of the London Underground's listed stations) it was, at 209 feet, London's first 'skyscraper' and the tallest secular building in the capital, a distinction which may have helped to earn it a sinister place in the world of literature. Graham Greene worked there briefly during the Second World War for the Intelligence Service and it is featured in his novel *The Ministry of Fear*, which was made into a film noir by Fritz Lang in 1944. It was also the model for the even more sinister 'Ministry of Truth', the workplace of Winston Smith in George Orwell's *1984*, where Smith concocts lies to conceal the truth from the inhabitants of Oceania. The Senate House was used as the Ministry of Truth in the film of *1984*, made in that year, with John Hurt and Richard Burton.

A short distance to the west is Tottenham Court Road which is, to this day, noted for its furniture shops, and it was in a shop in this street that furniture belonging to Traddles in *David Copperfield* was found after it had been seized from Micawber's house by one of his numerous creditors.

CANONBURY AND HOLLOWAY

To the north, at No. 5 Canonbury Place, was the home of the brothers George and Weedon Grossmith, both comic actors, who wrote and illustrated the comic novel *Diary of a Nobody*, published in 1892 and greatly admired by Evelyn Waugh who himself lived nearby at No. 17a Canonbury Square. The *Diary of a Nobody*, despite its unassuming title, is one of the funniest books ever written, being supposedly the diary of Charles Pooter, a lower-middle-class city clerk who lives at The Laurels, Brickfield Terrace, Holloway, a little to the north of the Grossmiths' home and an area which in the 1890s was expanding rapidly to accommodate families like the Pooters. Brickfield Terrace does not exist, but houses on Holloway Road are very similar to 'The Laurels' as described in *The Diary*: 'Six-roomed residence plus basement … a flight of ten steps up to the front door.' Pooter, having noted that the diaries of others are published, explains his decision to keep a diary:

> Why should I not publish my diary? I have often seen reminiscences of people I have never even heard of and I fail to see – because I do not happen to be a 'Somebody' – why my diary should not be interesting. My only regret is that I did not commence it when I was a youth.

The diary is a hilarious account of Mr Pooter's humiliations at the hands of a cast of miscellaneous characters, including his loving but critical wife Carrie, tradesmen, servants, casual acquaintances, readers of *Bicycle News*, conmen and, above all, his wayward son Lupin Pooter. Charles Pooter, whose meagre sense of humour is overshadowed by his sense of dignity and self-importance, is quite unaware of these humiliations and in the end he triumphs, informing the incorrigible Lupin: 'My boy, as a result of 21 years' industry and strict attention to the interests of my superiors in office, I have been rewarded with promotion and a rise in salary of £100.'

Reginald Wilfer, in Dickens's last completed novel, *Our Mutual Friend* (1865), has much in common with Mr Pooter as Wilfer, also a resident of Holloway, is, like Pooter, hen-pecked by his wife. But Holloway, by the time of Mr Pooter, has come a long way since it was the home of the Wilfers where it was: 'A suburban Sahara, where tiles and bricks were burnt, bones were boiled, carpets were beat, rubbish was shot, dogs were fought, and dust was heaped by contractors.'

Dickens placed Tommy Traddles from *David Copperfield* in Camden for a while, in a house very similar to the Dickens's home in Camden's Bayham Street, and the reader detects a sharp note of disapproval:

> I found that the street was not as desirable a one as I would have wished it to be, for the sake of Traddles. The inhabitants appeared to have a propensity to throw any trifles they were not in want of into the road which not only made it rank and sloppy but untidy too, on account of the cabbage leaves.

Likewise the Toodle family live in 'a little row of houses with little squalid patches of ground before them' in Staggs Gardens, Camden Town, an imaginary street built by a speculative builder to take advantage of the desire of the lower middle classes to move out from the grimy centre of London to what were then suburbs accessible via the rapidly growing railway network.

HAMPSTEAD & HIGHGATE

Much of *David Copperfield* is set in Highgate where Dickens and his parents lived for a while in 1832 and in whose famous cemetery his parents, and his daughter Dora, are buried. In *David Copperfield*, the former home of the villainous Steerforth and the home of his mother has been identified as Church House in South Grove, and it is to a home in Highgate that David Copperfield brings his empty-headed bride Dora Spenlow:

> I went into a cottage that I saw was to let and examined it narrowly, for I felt it necessary to be practical. It would do for me and Dora admirably: with a little front garden for Jip [Dora's spoilt dog] to run about and bark at the tradespeople through the railings.

The Spaniards Inn in Hampstead played host to Van Helsing in Bram Stoker's *Dracula* and was where Mrs Bardell plotted to trap Samuel Pickwick in Dickens' *The Pickwick Papers*. (Ewan Munro)

Eventually he decides to take a nearby house and here they are joined, in a nearby cottage, by his devoted aunt Betsey Trotwood. Such dwellings may still be seen.

Highgate is also featured in *Bleak House*, since it is at the Archway Toll that Inspector Bucket, employed first by the rascally Tulkinghorn and later by Sir Leicester Dedlock, picks up the trail of Lady Dedlock on her fatal flight from what she conceives to be disgrace since she believes, wrongly, that her devoted husband Sir Leicester will disown her when he discovers that before she met him she gave birth to an illegitimate daughter.

Highgate was also the childhood home of John Betjeman and he wrote of it with great warmth in 'Summoned by Bells':

Safe, in a world of trains and buttered toast
Where things inanimate could feel and think,
Deeply I loved thee, 31 West Hill!
At that hill's foot did London then begin,
With yellow horse-trams clopping past the planes
To grey-brick nonconformist Chetwynd Road
And on to Kentish town and barking dogs
And costers' carts and crowded grocers' shops
And Daniels' store, the local Selfridge's

Neighbouring Hampstead has literary associations of its own. The Spaniards Inn in Hampstead Lane dates from the sixteenth century and was, according to Dickens, the place where Mrs Bardell and her accomplices plotted to enmesh Samuel Pickwick in the breach of promise case which resulted in his temporary incarceration in the Fleet Prison. The Spaniards can also boast an appearance in Bram Stoker's *Dracula*, when Van Helsing and his gang retire to the inn after killing Lucy Westenra. The ponds on the neighbouring Heath are the subject of Samuel Pickwick's paper, 'Speculations on the Source of the Hampstead Ponds'. The inn also claims to be the place where John Keats, who lived nearby, composed 'Ode to a Nightingale'. Keats lived in what is now Keats Grove for the last five years of his life and composed much of his finest poetry there as well as contracting the tuberculosis from which he died in Rome in 1821. Keats's house, the poet's home, was completely restored in the 1970s and is now a museum.

A short walk to the west is Heath Street which was the home of the Upper Flask Tavern, used by Samuel Richardson (1689–1761) as a setting for some of the scenes in *Clarissa* (1748), one of the first novels ever written, whose formidable length (eight volumes) makes it more admired than read by modern readers. The tavern was also the home of the Kit Kat Club, which flourished from 1700–20 and included William Congreve and Joseph Addison amongst its members. The tavern itself no longer exists but its site is marked by Flask Walk, close to Hampstead station.

Hampstead also features in a dramatic episode in *Oliver Twist* and it is still possible to follow much of the route of Bill Sikes as he flees from London after murdering Nancy:

> He went through Islington; strode up the hill to Highgate on which there stands the stone in honour of Whittington [which may still be seen]; turned down Highgate Hill, unsteady of purpose and uncertain where to go; struck off to the right again, almost as soon as he began to descend it; and taking the footpath across the fields, skirted Caen Wood and so came out on Hampstead Heath. Traversing the hollow by the Vale of Health he mounted the opposite bank, and crossing the road which joins the villages of Hampstead and Highgate, made along the remaining portion of the heath to the fields at North End, in one of which he laid himself down under a hedge and slept.

Dickens himself lived for a short time in North End at Wylde's Farm, close to the site of North End station (the only station on the Underground system which was never opened because campaigners led by Henrietta Barnett secured the Heath against development).

John Betjeman spent much of his time in his youth on Hampstead Heath, contemplating his future as a poet rather than in the family cabinet-making business which his father had in mind (as recorded in Chapter 3). In his autobiographical work 'Summoned by Bells', Betjeman described his early struggles with his vocation:

> And so, at sunset, off to Hampstead Heath
> I went with pencil and with writing-pad
> And stood tip-toe upon a little hill,
> Awaiting inspiration from the sky.
> 'Look! there's a poet!', people might exclaim
> On footpaths near. The muse inspired my pen:
> The sunset tipped with gold St. Michael's church,
> Shouts of boys bathing came from Highgate Ponds,
> The elms that hid the houses of the great
> Rustled with mystery, and dirt-grey sheep
> Grazed in the foreground; but the lines of verse
> Came out like parodies of A & M.
> The gap between my feelings and my skill
> Was so immense, I wonder I went on.

Hampstead is also the place where the narrator meets the Woman in White in Wilkie Collins's novel of that name:

> I had now arrived at that particular point of my walk where four roads met – the road to Hampstead along which I had returned; the road to Finchley; the road to West End; and the road back to London. I had mechanically turned in this latter direction and was strolling along the lonely high road … when, in one moment, every drop of blood in my body was brought

> to a stop by the touch of a hand laid lightly and suddenly on my shoulder from behind me. I turned on the instant, with my fingers tightening round the handle of my stick. There, in the middle of the broad, bright high-road – there, as if it had at that moment sprung out of the earth or dropped from the heaven – stood the figure of a solitary Woman, dressed from head to foot in white garments …

No. 70 Queens' Avenue, Finchley, bears a commemorative tablet recording the fact that Charles Dickens stayed there in 1843 while writing *The Adventures of Martin Chuzzlewit* when the site was occupied by Cobley's Farm. It was there that he conceived the character of the gin-swilling midwife Mrs Gamp, whose umbrella gave rise to the expression 'a gamp' for an ill-kept example of that useful artefact.

Kensington Gardens, where J.M Barrie set one of his *Peter Pan* stories. (Mark Beynon)

7

HYDE PARK AND KENSINGTON & CHELSEA

John Galsworthy, early in *The Forsyte Saga*, signals the domestic status of members of the Forsyte family by telling the reader in considerable detail where each of them lives. The Forsyte aversion to Soho is noted elsewhere but the rest of the family may be found near Hyde Park, some in Mayfair, others in what is now the royal borough of Kensington & Chelsea:

> There was Old Jolyon in Stanhope Place; the James in Park Lane; Swithin in the lonely glory of orange and blue chambers in Hyde Park mansions – he had never married, not he! – the Soameses in their nest in Knightsbridge, the Rogers in Princes Gardens.

Soames's sister Winifred lives in a rented house in Green Street, off Park Lane, while Soames and Irene, following their wedding, begin their doomed marriage at No. 62 Montpelier Square. The square is a short walk from Harrods but No. 62, sadly, does not exist except in the writer's imagination.

In the slightly less grand Gloucester Square, Bayswater, to the north of Hyde Park, is the town house of Lady Monk in Trollope's *Can You Forgive Her*, the first of his Palliser novels. It is from here that Lady Glencora plans to elope with her wastrel lover Burgo Fitzgerald, a plot which is foiled by the timely arrival of Plantagenet Palliser with whom she is eventually to enjoy a happy marriage.

J.M. Barrie set one of his Peter Pan stories, *Peter Pan in Kensington Gardens*, in the gardens where Barrie himself liked to walk and where the Peter Pan statue now stands.

Matthew Arnold, in his 'Lines Written in Kensington Gardens' (1852) describes a place of tranquillity where he is screened from 'the girdling city's hum':

> In this lone, open glade I lie,
> Screen'd by deep boughs on either hand;
> And at its end, to stay the eye,
> Those black-crown'd, red-boled pine-trees stand!
> Birds here make song, each bird has his,
> Across the girdling city's hum.
> How green under the boughs it is!
> How thick the tremulous sheep-cries come!
> Sometimes a child will cross the glade
> To take his nurse his broken toy;
> Sometimes a thrush flit overhead
> Deep in her unknown day's employ.

Ezra Pound lived for a while in Kensington and in his poem 'The Garden' he wrote:

> Like a skein of loose silk blown against a wall
> She walks by the railing of a path in Kensington Gardens
> And she is dying piecemeal
> Of a sort of emotional anaemia.

A short distance to the west is Pitt Street, W8, which features as a crime scene in Sherlock Holmes's *The Adventure of the Six Napoleons*. Conan Doyle often used fictional addresses (e.g. 221B Baker Street) in his works but Pitt Street, Kensington, remains as he described it: 'a quiet little backwater just beside one of the briskest currents of London life.'

BROMPTON ROAD

To the south, on the corner of the Brompton Road and Boltons Place, is Bousfield Primary School, opened in 1956. It stands on the site of the childhood home of Beatrix Potter (1866–1943), where the young woman spent a lonely childhood with snobbish and zealously protective parents. She comforted herself by drawing pictures of plants (becoming a recognised authority on fungi) and animals, and it was the latter which inspired her to write her books, beginning with *The Tale of Peter Rabbit*, published by Warne in 1902 and soon followed by a series of titles which brought her greater sales than any other author of children's books at that time. She became engaged to her publisher Norman Warne in 1905 (against the wishes of her parents who objected to the fact that he was 'in trade'), but tragically he died shortly afterwards. Beatrix eventually moved to the Lake District where, with the proceeds of her books, she bought 4,000 acres of farmland to protect them from over-development and married a local solicitor called William Heelis. Her mother, of course, disapproved. But it was here, in the prosperous London area called The Boltons, that Peter Rabbit, Squirrel Nutkin, Pigling Bland and her other characters were first conceived.

In the same area, at about the same time, lived the Wilcox and Schlegel families of E.M. Forster's novel *Howard's End*. They lived in the fictional Wickham Place, the Schlegel family's house being:

> … fairly quiet, for a lofty promontory of buildings separated it from the main thoroughfare [i.e. Brompton Road]. One had the sense of a backwater, or rather of an estuary, whose waters flowed in from the invisible sea and ebbed into a profound silence while the waves without were still beating. Though the promontory consisted of flats – expensive, with cavernous entrance halls, full of concierge and palms – it fulfilled its purpose, and gained for the older houses opposite a certain measure of peace.

The flat in 'Wickham Mansions' occupied by the more commercially minded Wilcox family thus acts as a protective shield for the more sensitive and aesthetic Schlegels, the destinies of the two families becoming intertwined with tragic consequences. Many of the streets behind Brompton Road still have this combination of flats and older, more elegant houses.

Ranelagh Gardens in Chelsea opened in 1742 as a place of respectable entertainment, with an ornamental lake, booths for drinking tea and wine, a Chinese pavilion and an orchestra stand where Mozart played during a visit to London. Admission cost *2s 6d* (12½p, tea and coffee included) which excluded all but the well-to-do. In *The Expedition of Humphry Clinker*, Tobias Smollett described it as 'the enchanted palace of a genius … crowded with the great, the rich, the gay, the happy and the fair'. Edward Gibbon considered it 'the most convenient place for courtships of every kind' and Canaletto painted it. It closed in 1803 and was incorporated in the grounds of the Royal Hospital, Chelsea at the eastern side, adjacent to Chelsea Bridge Road.

THE CHELSEA EMBANKMENT

To the west, on the banks of the Thames, is Cheyne Walk, long the home of Thomas Carlyle (1795–1881) and close by, on its corner with Danvers Street, is Sir Thomas More's House, Crosby Place (which was referred to in Chapter 3) and relocated here in 1908.

A statue of the author of *Utopia* may be seen in the grounds of Chelsea Old Church on the corner of Old Church Street and the Chelsea Embankment. The church, close to the present site of Crosby House, dates from the fourteenth century and contains many mementoes to Sir Thomas More. He rebuilt the south chapel in 1528 for his own private worship and his first wife is buried here together with a tribute to Alice, his second wife and her devotion to his children from his first marriage:

> To them such love was by Alicia shown
> In stepmothers, a virtue rarely known,
> The world believed the children were her own.

In his novel *Murphy*, published in 1938, Samuel Beckett refers to the clock of Chelsea Old Church which 'ground out grudgingly the hour of ten', no doubt heard during Beckett's stay in London in the 1930s.

A short distance to the north, in Sydney Street across the King's Road, is St Luke's church, a magnificent neo-Gothic building constructed in the 1820s because Chelsea Old Church was too small for the growing population of Chelsea. Charles Dickens married Catherine Hogarth in this church on 2 April 1836, the rector being the brother of the Duke of Wellington.

SLOANE STREET

A short distance to the east, along the King's Road, is Radnor Walk where Sir John Betjeman lived after moving from Cloth Fair in 1972, and he set a number of his poems in the area. He sometimes worshipped at Holy Trinity, Sloane Street,

Holy Trinity in Sloane Street was where John Betjeman worshipped. (Amanda Slater)

close to Sloane Square Underground station, which was built in 1888–91 by the Victorian architect John Sedding. It is a striking example of the Arts and Crafts style, with stained glass by William Morris and Edward Burne-Jones. Damaged by incendiary bombs in the Second World War, it was restored but its huge size (it is actually wider than St Paul's Cathedral) led the Church Commissioners to propose demolishing it and replacing it with a smaller building. John Betjeman led a successful campaign to preserve it and it now thrives with a large congregation and a strong reputation for fine music. The building is worth visiting for its own sake, its architecture celebrated in Betjeman's poem 'Holy Trinity Sloane Street':

The tall red house soars upward to the stars,
The doors are chased with sardonyx and gold,
And in the long white room
Thin drapery draws backward to unfold
Cadogan square between the window bars
And Whistler's mother knitting in the gloom.

Cadogan Square, nearby, is the site of the Cadogan Hotel (75 Sloane Street) which is remembered as the site of Oscar Wilde's arrest following his unsuccessful attempt to sue the Marquess of Queensberry for slander. That event, too, was marked by Betjeman's poem 'The Arrest of Oscar Wilde at the Cadogan Hotel':

Mr Woilde, we 'ave come to tew take yew
Where felons and criminals dwell;
We must ask yew tew leave with us quoietly
For this is the Cadogan Hotel.

STAMFORD BRIDGE

Further to the west is Stamford Bridge, the home of Chelsea Football Club, which in July 2005 was featured in a book called *Incendiary* by the novelist Chris Cleave. It takes the form of a correspondence with Osama Bin Laden and culminates in a terrorist attack on a football match between the London rivals Chelsea and Arsenal in which many are killed, including the narrator's young son. The publication of the book was much heralded, not least by posters on Underground stations, and scheduled for 7 July. As London celebrated the award of the 2012 Olympics to London, announced on the day before the launch of *Incendiary*, fiction became fact as four suicide bombers launched attacks on the Underground and bus network, killing fifty-two Londoners and injuring many more. The posters were hastily removed and the publication of the book delayed, though it was eventually published with success and became a feature film.

HANS PLACE

In 1813–14 Jane Austen stayed at No. 23 Hans Place, Knightsbridge (marked by a Blue Plaque) and it was during this time that she was invited to Carlton House to meet an admirer of her writings, the Prince Regent, who suggested that she might dedicate *Emma* to him. This 'honour' was received with some misgivings by the author who had written critically of the Prince's treatment of his wife, Princess Charlotte, though the latter's marital behaviour was not without blemish since she travelled around Europe with a young Italian lover for company. Following a long and often amusing correspondence with Mr Clarke, the Prince's librarian, they agreed on the following wording:

To His Royal Highness, the Prince Regent,

This work is, by His Royal Highness's Permission

Most respectfully dedicated

By his Royal Highness's Dutiful and Obedient Humble Servant,

THE AUTHOR

8

THE EAST END

Dickens makes comparatively few references to the industrial and commercial life of London, though two of his novels, *Dombey and Son* and *Our Mutual Friend*, have several episodes set in the heart of London's dockland. In *Dombey and Son* Captain Cuttle 'lived on the brink of a little canal near the India docks, where there was a swivel bridge which opened now and then to let some wandering monster of a ship to come wandering up the street like a stranded Leviathan'. Captain Cuttle's home could be almost anywhere on the Isle of Dogs and if he were living there now he would presumably be living in one of the luxury flats, his yacht moored in one of the marinas into which the old docks have been transformed. He would be working in one of the banks whose skyscrapers dominate the landscape. He might occasionally see Lizzie Hexam, from *Our Mutual Friend*, rowing along the river with her father Gaffer, a Thames waterman who makes his living by finding and robbing corpses that he drags from the river. Gaffer lives on the river bank at Limehouse, as does his fellow scavenger (and competitor) Rogue Riderhood. Gaffer's house is conical in shape and looks like a derelict windmill which has lost its sails.

Limehouse Basin, a marina with a lock which connects the Regent's Canal to the Thames, is now the home of flats and luxury yachts, and separated from the river by Narrow Street in which, at No. 76, is located a riverside pub called 'The Grapes'. It has been on this site since 1720 and has resisted all attempts to subject it to the redevelopment which has overwhelmed this part of London. It has been identified by some as the model for Dickens's 'The Six Jolly Fellowship Porters', not least because of stories that watermen, like Gaffer Hexam, would drown drunks in the river, empty their pockets and then sell their corpses for dissection by medical schools. In tribute, 'The Grapes' now has a 'Dickens Bar'.

SHOREDITCH

The East End was also the subject of writers concerned with London's impoverished and criminal classes. E.A. Morrison's book *Child of the Jago*, published in 1896, was based on the 'Old Nichol' slum to the east of Shoreditch High Street, its former site now marked by Old Nichol Street. The author, Arthur Morrison (1863–1945), was born in nearby Poplar and wrote from experience, claiming in his preface to the novel that he had in mind 'a place in Shoreditch, where children were born and reared in circumstances which gave them no reasonable chance of living decent lives: where they were born foredamned to a criminal or semi-criminal career'. The central character, Dicky Perrott, is the son of a weak mother and a ne'er-do-well, drunken father. Dicky is led into a life of crime working for Arthur Weech, a Fagin-like figure who employs children to steal for him. Dicky is told that he has to choose between gaol, the gallows, or becoming one of the 'Igh Mob', the successful criminals whose rival gangs dominate the Jago in an atmosphere reminiscent of the influence in the area of the Krays in the 1950s and 1960s.

At the time that Morrison's book appeared there worked in the area the Revd Arthur Osborne Jay (1858–1945), vicar of Holy Trinity Church, Shoreditch, who turned his church into a refuge for the homeless and a youth and sports club for young, rootless people. In *Child of the Jago* Jay appears as Friar Sturt, whose attempts to rescue Dicky from his life of crime are frustrated by Weech. Dicky is eventually killed during a gang fight at the age of 17. Morrison's work was much criticised at the time for its uncompromising account of life in one of London's most deprived areas, one critic claiming: 'The original of the Jago has, it is admitted, ceased to exist. But I will make bold to say that, as described by Mr Morrison, it never did exist.' Yet the work of Henry Mayhew, published in *London Labour and the London Poor* and later of Charles Booth, *Life and Labour of the People of London* showed that Morrison's account, though fictional, reflected reality. And the impact of the novel was such that the terms 'Nichol' and 'Jago' became synonyms.

Bethnal Green was, for a while, the home of Sikes and Nancy in *Oliver Twist*. Much of the area was destroyed by bombing or demolished in slum clearance measures after 1945, but many of the streets mentioned in Morrison's work, notably Old Nichol Street, Boundary Street, Bethnal Green Road and Shoreditch High Street, may still be seen. Morrison also wrote a series of articles and stories on similar themes for *Macmillan's Magazine* which were later published as *Tales of Mean Streets*.

Matthew Arnold, whose verses on Kensington Gardens have been noted, wrote less flatteringly of Bethnal Green and of the fate of impoverished silk weavers in Spitalfields in his poem 'East London':

> 'Twas August, and the fierce sun overhead
> Smote on the squalid streets of Bethnal Green,
> And the pale weaver, through his windows seen
> In Spitalfields looked twice dispirited.

Samuel Pickwick made one of his rare excursions to the East End when he and his companions visited the United Grand

Junction Ebenezer Temperance Association, which was to be found in Brick Lane, Shoreditch.

Brick Lane itself gives its name to the title of Monica Ali's novel *Brick Lane*, with its rather unflattering portrait of the Bangladeshi community which predominates in the area. Shortlisted for the Man Booker Prize in 2003, Germaine Greer was amongst those who criticised the book, claiming that it had created 'a defining caricature' of part of the Bangladeshi community. The book was made into a film in 2007.

WHITECHAPEL

South of Shoreditch, in the Whitechapel area of Tower Hamlets, was a building which features in the works of Jack London (1876–1916) and George Orwell (1903–50). This was Tower House, which was built by the philanthropist Montagu William Lowry-Corry (1838–1903), a grandson of the Earl of Shaftesbury from whom he perhaps inherited his philanthropic genes. Lowry-Corry worked as private secretary to Benjamin Disraeli and was made Baron Rowton in 1880 when Disraeli left office. In 1890 Rowton donated £30,000 of his considerable fortune to build and run decent lodging houses for working men, providing such luxuries as clean sheets, hot baths and laundry facilities. The best known 'Rowton House' was in Fieldgate Street, Whitechapel. Jack London was one of its early residents and in his work *The People of the Abyss* he described it as 'the Monster Doss House' and wrote that it was 'full of life that was degrading and unwholesome'. George Orwell, in *Down and Out in Paris and London* was much more appreciative, recording that:

> The best lodging houses are the Rowton houses where the charge is a shilling, for which you get a cubicle to yourself and the use of excellent bathrooms. You can

> also pay half a crown for a special, which is practically hotel accommodation. The Rowton houses are splendid buildings and the only objection to them is the strict discipline with rules against cooking, card-playing etc.

Tower House still exists at No. 81 Fieldgate Street, E1, behind the East London mosque, though it has now been converted into luxury flats. The only Rowton house still in use as a lodging house is Arlington House in Camden. Situated at 220 Arlington Road, it has recently been extensively refurbished and was for a time the home of the Irish writer Brendan Behan.

9

WHERE TAXIS DON'T GO: SOUTH OF THE RIVER

The humorous expression sometimes attributed to taxi drivers, 'I don't go south of the river', may be traced back to a decision of Oliver Cromwell. In 1654 he licensed the 'Fellowship of Master Hackney Coachmen' who, in return for an annual licence fee of £5, enjoyed a monopoly of four-wheeled transport north of the Thames as far as the 'New Road' which is now the line of the Marylebone Road–Euston Road–Pentonville Road–City Road route. They enjoyed no such privileges south of the river which probably suited them since it had been a disreputable area to which undesirable people and activities had been banished by the authorities. Since, besides bear-baiting and prostitution, these included actors and theatres, the area south of the river, especially Southwark, is rich in literary connections, not least with William Shakespeare.

SOUTHWARK

Much of Little Dorrit is set in Southwark. The Marshalsea Prison for debtors, where John Dickens was confined during Charles's time at the blacking factory, was for so long the 'home' of William Dorrit that he was known as 'The Father of the Marshalsea'.

John Dickens (1785–1851) was the well-meaning but improvident father of the novelist, whose inability to manage his finances resulted in his incarceration in the Marshalsea Prison for debtors, in Southwark, and Charles's despatch to Warren's Blacking Warehouse near Hungerford Market, Charing Cross. It was later moved to Bedford Street, to the north of the Strand where Dickens's humiliation was aggravated by his having to work in public view, applying labels to bottles. The shame of his father's humiliation and his spell in the blacking warehouse haunted Dickens for the rest of his life, but did not prevent him from drawing on the experiences in his novels. The kind, optimistic but helpless Wilkins Micawber in *David Copperfield* is a thinly disguised portrait of John Dickens. However, Micawber would not have had John's effrontery in approaching the novelist's publisher, Chapman and Hall, to ask for a loan following the success of *Pickwick Papers*. No. 16 Bayham Street, Camden Town was one of John's many homes and was the model for Bob Cratchit's home in *A Christmas Carol* and for Traddles's lodgings with Micawber. It has since been demolished but the site is marked by a plaque.

Dorrit was the victim of an uncompleted contract with the Circumlocution Office, a portrait of officialdom and the legal system which rivals *Bleak House* in its bitter satire. In *Little Dorrit* the reader can feel the memory of Dickens's childhood experience as he describes the prison:

> Thirty years ago there stood, a few doors short of the church of Saint George, in the Borough of Southwark, on the left hand side of the way going southward, the

> Marshalsea Prison. It had stood there many years before and it remained there some years afterwards; but it is gone now, and the world is none the worse without it.

Dickens's description of the Marshalsea in *Little Dorrit* was written in 1857, fifteen years after the jail was demolished, but his recollection of it during his family's incarceration there in 1824 is clear and harsh:

> It was an oblong pile of barrack building, partitioned into squalid houses standing back to back, so that there were no back rooms; environed by a narrow paved yard; hemmed in by high walls duly spiked on top.

In a preface to *Little Dorrit,* written shortly after the story had been completed, Dickens described how he had recently visited the site of the prison: 'Whosoever goes into Marshalsea Court, turning out of Angel Court, leading to Bermondsey, will find his feet on the very paving stones of the extinct Marshalsea jail ... and will stand upon the crowding ghosts of many miserable years.' The streets have been somewhat altered since 1857 but the pedestrian can easily find Angel Place, as it is now called, Marshalsea Road and Little Dorrit Court, Angel Place being the site of a plaque fixed to the wall which used to mark the southern boundary of the prison. We can tread in Dickens's footsteps but we can scarcely feel as he did as he visited a place he remembered with shame and horror until his death. So inured is William Dorrit to life in the Marshalsea that when he inherits a fortune and leaves the prison he has difficulty adapting to life outside and he dies in Rome on a continental tour following his release.

A little to the south of the Marshalsea, at the junction of Borough Road and Borough High Street, lay another debtors' prison, the King's Bench, to which Dickens sent Wilkins Micawber during one of his many brushes with financial embarrassment. There David Copperfield visited him and found Micawber ready to give birth to one of the most famous passages in the language:

> Mr Micawber was waiting for me within the gate, and we went up to his room (top storey but one) and cried very much. He solemnly conjured me to take warning by his fate; and to observe that if a man had twenty pounds a year for his income and spent nineteen pounds nineteen shillings and sixpence he would be happy but that if he spent twenty pounds one he would be miserable. After which he borrowed a shilling off me for porter.

Just a little further to the south again, at the junction of Newington Causeway and Harper Road, is the Inner London Crown Court which stands on the site of the former Horsemonger Lane Jail.

Marshalsea Prison in Southwark was where Dickens sent the Dorrit family and Samuel Pickwick. It was also where his father, John Dickens, was committed. (Mark Beynon)

There, in 1849, Dickens was amongst a crowd who witnessed the execution of a married couple, George Manning and his Swiss wife Maria, who had murdered a former lover of Maria and buries the corpse, in quicklime, beneath their kitchen floor. Maria's attempts to escape the consequences of a crime in which she had clearly been involved shocked the public, the execution drawing a crowd of 30,000 whose behaviour, 'the shrillness of the cries and howls that were raised from time to time', shocked Dickens. He may have drawn on his knowledge of the case to portray the murderous maid Hortense, in *Bleak House* who, like Maria Manning, was both foreign (French) and a former maid. The gravestones of the Mannings are now on display in the nearby Cuming Museum and Library in the Walworth Road.

Just across Borough High Street, running parallel to Marshalsea Road, is Lant Street, which was for a time the home of both Charles Dickens and of the hero of his autobiographical novel, *David Copperfield*, the latter commemorated by Copperfield Street which stretches beyond Marshalsea Road. Mr and Mrs Garland in *The Old Curiosity Shop* are believed to be based on the author's Lant Street landlord and his wife. Samuel Pickwick and his companions also enjoy the supper party given by the Guy's Hospital medical student Bob Sawyer in his Lant Street lodgings. Dickens who, despite his father's embarrassments, appears to have been very attached to the area and its residents, gave an affectionate portrait of the area in *The Pickwick Papers*:

> There is a repose about Lant Street which sheds a gentle melancholy upon the soul … The chief features in the still life of the street are green shutters, lodging bills, brass doorplates and bell-handles; the principal specimens of animated nature the pot boy, the muffin youth and the baked potato man. The population is migratory, usually disappearing on the verge of quarterday [i.e. when rent was due] and usually by night. Her Majesty's revenues are seldom collected in this happy valley; the rents are dubious and the water is very frequently cut off.

Other Dickens characters are also celebrated in street names including Trundle Street and Weller Street (both from *The Pickwick Papers*) as well as Little Dorrit Court and the church of St George the Martyr where Little Dorrit was finally married to Arthur Clennam and where she is commemorated in the church's 'Little Dorrit' East Window. The ending of *Little Dorrit*, one of the most moving that Dickens wrote, tells how, at the end of the marriage ceremony, husband and wife:

> Walked out of the church alone. They paused for a moment on the steps of the portico, looking at the fresh perspective of the street in the autumn morning sun's bright rays, and then went down. Went down into a modest life of usefulness and happiness … They went quietly down into the roaring streets, inseparable and blessed; and as they passed along in sunshine and in shade, the noisy and the eager, and the arrogant and the forward and the vain fretted and chafed and made their usual uproar.

PILGRIMS AND POETS

The George Inn, off Borough High Street, also features in *Little Dorrit* and survives as London's only galleried inn. It is sometimes (mistakenly) identified as the Tabard Inn from which Chaucer's pilgrims set out in The Prologue to the *Canterbury Tales*:

> It happened that in that season, on a day
> In Southwark, at the Tabard as I lay
> Ready to go on pilgrimage and start
> To Canterbury, full devout at heart,
> There came at nightfall to that hostelry
> Some nine and twenty in a company
> Of sundry persons who had chanced to fall
> In fellowship and pilgrims were they all
> That toward Canterbury town would ride.
> The rooms and stables spacious were and wide
> And well we there were eased and of the best

The verse reads almost like an advertisement for the inn!

The original Tabard certainly existed, along with its landlord, Harry Bailey. It was burned to the ground in 1676 and rebuilt as The Talbot, which retained the original gallery to be used by visiting theatrical troupes, especially during Southwark Fair which flourished from the fifteenth to the eighteenth century and was celebrated in Hogarth's 1733 engraving of the event. The landlord of the renamed inn, presumably fearing that he was losing trade as a result of the name change, placed a placard across the entrance informing visitors that 'This is the Inn where Sir Jeffrey Chaucer and the nine and twenty pilgrims lay in the journey to Canterbury, anno 1383'. The poet's ghost was no doubt grateful for the knighthood posthumously conferred along with the name change, but it didn't save the inn which was finally demolished in 1873. Its name is preserved on its original site, Talbot Yard, off Borough High Street on the approach to London Bridge. The George Inn nearby serves as a suitable proxy and was probably one of the coaching inns Dickens had in mind in *The Pickwick Papers* when he wrote of 'great, rambling, queer old places with galleries and passages and staircases'.

The most prominent building in Southwark is Southwark Cathedral. Begun in 1220, it is the oldest Gothic church in London, having escaped the fire which consumed the City churches, on the opposite bank of the Thames, in 1666. It was originally a parish church, St Saviour's, and did not become a cathedral until the new diocese of Southwark was carved out of the diocese of Winchester in 1897. It contains the tomb of Lancelot Andrewes, Bishop of Winchester, and one of the principal translators of the Authorised ('King James') version of the Bible which, with the plays of Shakespeare, is part of the architecture of the English language. On Christmas Day 1622, Lancelot Andrewes preached a sermon before King James himself at Whitehall Palace which, in reference to the three wise men who visited Christ, contained the words:

> A cold coming they had of it at this time of the year, just the worst time of the year to take a journey, and specially a long journey. The ways deep, the weather sharp, the days short, the sun farthest off.

These words were adopted and placed into the mouths of the Magi themselves by T.S. Eliot in the opening verse of his poem 'The Coming of the Magi', which the poet wrote at the time of his baptism and reception into the Anglican church in 1927:

> A cold coming we had of it,
> Just the worst time of the year
> For a journey, and such a journey:
> The ways deep and the weather sharp,
> The very dead of winter.
> And the camels galled, sore-footed, refractory,

The George Inn, off Borough High Street, is the only galleried inn left in London and was featured in *Little Dorrit*. (Ewan Munro)

Lying down in the melting snow.
There were times we regretted
The summer palaces on slopes, the terraces,
And the silken girls bringing sherbet.

THE GLOBE

Shakespeare himself, of course, has many associations with Southwark. Since theatres were banned from the City itself, as attracting undesirables like actors, they were built either outside the City precincts or in the particularly disreputable district across the river, on Bankside. The first was The Rose, which was built by Philip Henslowe, an impresario and entrepreneur, in 1587. Henslowe found brief fame when he was portrayed by Geoffrey Rush, in the film *Shakespeare in Love*, with a small part as 'The Apothecary' in *Romeo and Juliet*, a role for which the actor received an Oscar nomination. The Rose saw the first productions of Marlowe's *Tamburlaine* and Shakespeare's *Henry VI Part I*. Henslowe's theatre enjoyed so much success that it was soon followed, and eclipsed, by The Swan and The Globe nearby. The Rose's foundations were revealed during construction work in 1989 close to Southwark Bridge where there is now an exhibition.

The Globe was first built in 1576 close to the later site of The Curtain in what is now Curtain Road, Shoreditch. It was built by the actor James Burbage and prospered, but, following an argument with the owner of the land, Burbage and his company dismantled the theatre one night, moved it bodily across the river and re-erected it in 1599. One of the shareholders (and presumably therefore one of the removal men) was one William Shakespeare. Like many theatres of the time it had a relatively short life. It was destroyed by fire in 1613 during a performance of *Henry VIII* when two cannons were fired to welcome the arrival of the actor playing the king. The thatch caught fire and the theatre was destroyed. The only casualty was a man whose breeches caught fire and 'put it out with bottled ale'.

The present Shakespeare's Globe we owe to the American actor Sam Wanamaker, who was so moved by a replica of the original theatre which he saw as a young man at a fair in Chicago that he came to London to see the original. Learning that it had burned down three centuries earlier he set about reconstructing it, using the plans of the original theatre and, as far as possible, original materials (along with a few modern amenities like sprinkler systems). Its prominent site on Bankside is close to that of the original Globe whose foundations may be seen in the courtyard of some flats on Park Street nearby.

There was one notable exception to the 'no theatres in the City' rule and this exception was a source of great irritation to the City authorities, and to Shakespeare and his colleagues who were banished to the South Bank. In 1578 Richard Farrant, a composer of some fine church music which is still regularly performed, opened the Blackfriars Playhouse in his capacity as 'Master of the Children of the Chapel Royal'. He argued that it was a theatre where choristers could practise 'for the better training them to do her Majesty service'. Given his royal connections there was little the City fathers could do and when Farrant died in 1580 it was bought by James Burbage, father of the actor Richard Burbage, and turned into a private theatre, though it continued to be used by the choristers who, besides practising their singing, also performed plays. In *Hamlet* Act II scene II Shakespeare makes a bitter reference to 'an eyrie of children … these are now the fashion and so berattle the common stages'. Richard Burbage, in company with six fellow actors, one of whom was Shakespeare, eventually took over the running of the theatre for his company 'The King's Men', royal patronage once again helping to overcome any objections from the City. Many of Shakespeare's plays were performed there until the theatre was closed by the Puritans in 1642 and demolished in 1655. Its site, however, is marked by Playhouse Yard, off Blackfriars Lane.

LAMBETH

To the west of Southwark, in the borough of Lambeth, is Waterloo station, which features in Jerome K. Jerome's (1859–1927) *Three Men in a Boat (to say nothing of the Dog)*, published in 1889. The book begins with an account of the hypochondriac narrator's visit to the British Museum library to establish the cause of a mild illness: 'I remember going to the British Museum one day to read up for treatment for some slight ailment … the only malady I could conclude I had not got was housemaid's knee.' The three friends, Jerome, George, Harris and Montmorency (the dog), decide to row from Kingston to Oxford to restore their health and begin by going to Waterloo to take a train for Kingston:

> We saw the engine driver and asked him if he was going to Kingston. He said he couldn't know for certain of course but that he rather thought he was … We slipped half-a-crown into his hand and begged him to be the 11.15 for Kingston … 'I suppose some train's got to go to Kingston and I'll do it. Gimme the half-crown …' We learned afterwards that the train we had come by was really the Exeter mail and that they had spent hours at Waterloo looking for it.

(This claim of course overlooked the fact that it is the signalman, not the driver, who decides the destination of a train.)

Jerome's later work *Three Men on the Bummel* is set in Germany but begins just along the Thames from Waterloo where George stops to buy boots near Astley's amphitheatre, a circus venue at 225 Westminster Bridge Road where Robert Martin and Harriet Smith had earlier come to an understanding with each other out of reach of the well-meaning interference of Jane Austen's Emma who was determined to choose Harriet's husband on her behalf.

Jane Austen herself had visited the establishment in 1794. Jerome K. Jerome's narrator explains:

> We stopped the cab at a boot shop a little past Astley's theatre that looked the sort of place we wanted.
> It was one of those overfed shops that the moment their shutters are taken down in the morning disgorge their goods all round them. Boxes of boots stood piled on the pavement or in the gutter opposite.

When George asks if he can buy some boots the reaction of the proprietor is less than welcoming: 'What d'ye think I keep boots for, to smell 'em? Did you ever hear of a man keeping a boot shop and not selling boots? What d'ye take me for, a prize idiot?'

After visiting Bucklersbury, opposite the Bank of England in the heart of the City, to hire a yacht to take them to the Continent, the party returns to a small shop in the Blackfriars Road, east of Waterloo station, so that George can buy a cap. George explains to the shopkeeper that he wants 'A good cap'. Once again he receives a discouraging reply:

> Ah, there I am afraid you have me. Now if you had wanted a bad cap, not worth the price asked for it; a cap good for nothing but to clean windows with I could have found you the very thing. But a good cap – no, we don't keep them.

Poor George: bootless and capless.

To the south, still in the borough of Lambeth, is Walcot Square. Virtually unaltered since the time of Charles Dickens, it is in fact a triangle in which, in *Bleak House*, Mr Guppy leases 'a commodious tenement, a six-roomer' during his unsuccessful pursuit of the heroine of the novel, the saintly Esther Summerson.

Further to the west, still in Lambeth, is St Thomas's Hospital where, in the 1890s, Somerset Maugham worked as a medical student and junior doctor. This was an area noted for violent crime and Maugham left an account of his work in the area as he travelled, on foot, to some of its darkest areas to minister to the poor and, in particular, to deliver babies. He felt perfectly secure because he was protected by his 'Gladstone bag', a portmanteau which carried medical instruments and supplies and which was recognised as that of a doctor, a profession viewed with respect even in the poorest areas. Maugham's first novel, *Liza of Lambeth* (1897), draws on his experience. It is the story of Liza Kemp, a factory girl, the youngest of thirteen children, who enters into an adulterous relationship with Jim Blakeston, a 40-year-old married father of nine by whom Liza becomes pregnant. Domestic violence is a frequent occurrence in the lives of the characters, often fuelled by drink and one of the novel's most dramatic episodes occurs when Jim's wife attacks Liza, cheered on by a baying crowd of women. Liza dies following a miscarriage, an episode the young Somerset Maugham must often have witnessed. Liza's home is in Vere Street, a fictional street off Westminster Bridge Road with which the young doctor was thoroughly familiar.

007 AND FIREWORKS

To the south of Westminster Bridge Road is Vauxhall Cross, the headquarters of MI6 now standing brazenly on the banks of the Thames. Now the home of James Bond, 'M', 'Q' and the other characters made famous by the novels of Ian Fleming and the films which followed, the building did not exist in Fleming's lifetime (indeed MI6 itself, the Secret Intelligence Service (SIS), had no official existence until 1994). Fleming himself worked for the SIS during the Second World War when it was based at 54 Broadway, near St James's Park.

On the opposite side of the Albert Embankment from Vauxhall Cross is a small park called Spring Gardens, adjacent to Vauxhall station. This was once one of London's main centres of entertainment. Opened in about 1660 it became known in 1785 as Vauxhall Gardens and was furnished with Chinese pavilions, restaurants, tightrope walkers, discreet venues for assignations and entertainments such as firework displays, hot air balloon ascents and orchestras. In 1749 Handel's *Music for the Royal Fireworks* attracted an audience of 12,000 and Thomas Arne, composer of *Rule Britannia*, was the director of music there for thirty years from 1745. Tobias Smollett in *The Expedition of Humphry Clinker* referred to 'a composition of baubles, over-charged with paltry ornaments, ill-conceived and poorly-executed; without any unity of design or propriety of disposition' though he later relented and called it 'a place crowded with the gayest company, ranging through those blissful shades, or supping in different lodges on cold collations, enlivened with mirth, freedom and good humour, and animated by an excellent band of music.' Wordsworth, after a visit at the age of 18, wrote in *The Prelude, Book VII, Residence in London* of its:

> … green groves, and wilderness of lamps
> Dimming the stars, and fireworks magical,
> And gorgeous ladies, under splendid domes,
> Floating in dance, or warbling high in air
> The songs of spirits!

Thackeray, in *Vanity Fair*, makes the gardens the scene of one of Becky Sharp's failed attempts to trap the amiable, wealthy and indolent Jos Sedley into a proposal of marriage. In 1859 the gardens closed and the park we see at Vauxhall is a small relic of its former extensive grounds.

Broadway, St James's Park, was formerly home to the SIS and Ian Fleming throughout the Second World War. (Chris Sampson)

WANDSWORTH, HAMMERSMITH & FULHAM

Further to the south, in the borough of Wandsworth, is Wandsworth Prison, a prominent feature of Graham Greene's early work *It's a Battlefield* (1934), which the author describes as his 'first overtly political work'. It concerns the story of a Communist bus driver called Jim Drover, who stabs an undercover police officer who is about to hit Drover's wife at a Communist rally they are attending. Drover is condemned to hang and spends time in Wandsworth Prison where little is heard of him throughout the novel whose themes are more concerned with the implications of his sentence than the fate of the individual himself. As Greene himself said, the theme of the book is 'the injustice of man's justice' as Drover's Communist colleagues hope for his execution in the belief that its injustice will rouse the sympathy of the public. Greene visited a prison to inform his depiction of life inside its walls and a match factory so that he could describe such a factory where Drover's sister-in-law worked. The novel draws parallels between the lives of factory workers and those of prison inmates. He called the work 'a panoramic novel of London', the detective story being a vehicle by which he can explore the nature of class conflict, capitalism and politics. As in many of Greene's novels, few characters are ever happy for long.

Further to the west is Putney, which in the nineteenth century was a suburb of London. It was the home of Dora Spenlow in *David Copperfield* after the death of her father, where she was despatched to live with maiden aunts. Consequently the love-struck David spent many fruitless hours there, on one occasion walking there from the city with his friend Traddles in order to ingratiate himself with the two maiden ladies. The marriage of David and Dora eventually takes place and a reference to 'boatmen strolling in' to the church suggests that the building Dickens had in mind for the ceremony was Putney parish church, which lies on the riverside and is most often seen at the start of the Oxford and Cambridge Boat Race. On the opposite bank of the river is 'a pretty villa at Fulham, on the banks of the Thames, which was one of the most desirable residences in the world when a rowing-match happened to be going past'. This was the home of Sir Barnet and Lady Skettles in Dombey and Son where Florence Dombey stayed, walking along the river bank while she lamented her rejection by her father whose interest lay only in his son. The riverside villas are no more, but the most notable of them, Craven Cottage, which was the home of Dickens's friend and fellow author Edward Bulwer-Lytton, is remembered in the name of stadium of Fulham Football Club which overlooks the river.

Further along the river to the west, The Dove Inn at 19 Upper Mall, Hammersmith, opened as the Dove Coffee House in 1796 and is one of London's best known riverside inns. William Morris lived next door and the humorous writer A.P. Herbert used The Dove as a model for the pub The Pigeons in his novel *The Water Gypsies*. The Scottish writer James Thomson (1700–48) also wrote the words for *Rule Britannia* at The Dove, which is one of the most popular vantage points from which to watch the Oxford and Cambridge Boat Race.

GREENWICH

St Alphege's Church in Greenwich is a fine Baroque structure designed by Nicholas Hawksmoor in 1714 and sympathetically restored in 1953 after being bombed in 1941. This was the scene of the marriage of John Harmon and Bella Wilfer in *Our Mutual Friend*, the ceremony taking place without the knowledge of Bella's hostile mother. An earlier church saw the baptism of Henry VIII who was born in Greenwich.

The Trafalgar Tavern in Park Row, Greenwich, was patronised by many writers including Charles Dickens, W.M. Thackeray and Wilkie Collins and in *Our Mutual Friend* Dickens chose it for the wedding feast of Bella and John. It was noted for its fresh fish, particularly whitebait, and Dickens wrote: 'What a dinner! Specimens of all the fishes that swim in the sea surely had swum their way to it!' It was extensively used, also for 'Whitebait dinners', by Victorian cabinet ministers, the last official such dinner being celebrated by Gladstone's administration in 1880. In the 1980s the tradition was revived when a dining club called Saints and Sinners, comprising members of Mrs Thatcher's cabinet, resumed the practice of dining there. John and Bella move to a 'bright and fresh' cottage at Blackheath, an area familiar to Dickens as he would cross it on his way from his homes in London to Gad's Hill near Rochester.

At the opening of *A Tale of Two Cities* the Dover Mail is ascending Shooter's Hill, Blackheath, which was also, according to the author, the home of David Copperfield's hated school Salem House. In fact the school was almost certainly based upon Wellington House Academy in Mornington Crescent.

10

OUTER LONDON AND BEYOND

Literary associations are not, of course, confined to the relatively small part of inner London to which space has confined this work. Zadie Smith, for example, in her novel *White Teeth*, celebrates Willesden with its rich and ironic mixture of often bewildered members of different racial groups, political views and faiths. It gives a charming and optimistic account of a multicultural community, its personalities and events bathed in humour, its multilingual character described as 'Babelian'. It occupies an honoured place in a tradition stretching back to Chaucer.

Travelling further north-west we find Harrow, where Anthony Trollope went to school and lived in a farmhouse which became the model for his novel *Orley Farm*, the name of the novel having been adopted in the nineteenth century by the school which purchased Trollope's former home and still occupies the site. Byron also attended Harrow School, though his 'favourite spot' was in the churchyard where a marble plaque is engraved with a verse from his 'Lines written beneath an Elm'.

To the south, in Kingston-upon-Thames, the extensive childhood home of John Galsworthy, Coombe Leigh, was later occupied by a school and was the model for Robin

Hill in *The Forsyte Saga*, the home to which Soames planned to take his wife Irene in the hope of gaining her affection: a hope frustrated when she fell in love with the architect Philip Bosinney.

To the south-east, in Eltham, is the former home of Sir Thomas More's daughter Margaret Roper, which gave its name to Moat House, the home of E. Nesbit's Bastable family in her 1899 work *The Story of the Treasure Seekers*.

And one could venture further to Gravesend, in Kent, off whose shore Joseph Conrad's story *Heart of Darkness* is narrated on a boat lying in the Thames.

But all these, and much more, are for another time and another book …